Embodied AI Integration in Education

A Thoughtful Implementation Guide for Innovative Teaching

Johnna Haskell

Published by: Epic Leaf Innovations LLC

For permission requests, please contact the publisher at: epicleafinnovations.com

Hardcover: 978-1-964562-05-6

Paperback: 978-1-964562-04-9

EBook: B0DF98Z59W

Table of Contents

Introduction

After exploring the theoretical foundations in *Embodied AI Education: Unlocking Human Potential Through Enactive Learning*, we now turn theory into action. This journey begins with Ms. Chen's seventh-grade classroom, where students move naturally between physical and digital spaces, their movements and interactions seamlessly blending with artificial intelligence (AI)-supported learning. Her story, along with others you'll meet throughout this guide, illustrates how embodied AI implementation transforms from concept to reality.

This isn't just another technology integration manual. It's a collection of real experiences, practical wisdom, and proven strategies from educators who've navigated the path you're about to begin. Through their stories and lessons learned, you'll discover how to create learning environments where AI enhances rather than replaces the physical and social aspects of education.

Our purpose is threefold:

1. To show, through real classroom examples, how AI tools can enhance embodied, enactive learning

2. To guide you through curriculum redesign that leverages AI while maintaining focus on physical engagement

3. To help you navigate ethical considerations through the lens of actual implementation experiences

Each chapter follows educators at different stages of their AI implementation journey, offering practical insights through their successes and challenges. You'll meet

- veteran teachers discovering new possibilities in familiar practices

- first-year educators bringing fresh perspectives to AI integration

- administrators balancing innovation with practical constraints

- students whose natural interaction with technology offers valuable lessons

This guide is designed for active engagement. As you read about others' experiences, you'll find opportunities to

- reflect on your own teaching context

- experiment with implementation strategies

- connect with other educators on similar journeys

- adapt approaches to fit your unique environment

Remember, this journey isn't about perfecting AI implementation—it's about the thoughtful evolution of your teaching practice. Let these stories guide and inspire your own path toward creating learning experiences that combine the best of human wisdom with technological innovation.

Let's explore how embodied AI can enhance your educational practice while maintaining focus on what matters most—creating meaningful learning experiences that engage the whole person while fostering potential.

Chapter 1:

Preparing for Embodied AI

Integration

Integrating AI into your educational environment is both exciting and complex. It requires careful planning, thoughtful consideration, and a holistic approach that considers not just the technology but also the entire ecosystem of your school or institution. In this section, we'll walk through the crucial steps of preparing for AI integration, ensuring that you're set up for success from the very beginning.

Assessing Your Current Educational Environment

Before you can effectively integrate AI into your educational practice, it's essential to have a clear understanding of your current environment. This assessment will serve as the foundation for all your future AI integration efforts.

Begin by evaluating your existing technology infrastructure. Consider the quality and speed of your internet connection, the availability and condition of hardware such as computers and tablets, your current software and digital learning platforms, and the level of tech support available.

Next, assess the digital literacy levels of both your staff and students. Consider their comfort levels with existing technology, experience with

AI tools or applications, and willingness to learn and adapt to new technologies.

Reflect on your current pedagogical practices and how they align with embodied, enactive learning principles. Ask yourself how often you use project-based or experiential learning approaches, to what extent your current practices engage students' bodies as well as their minds, and how personalized your current approach to learning is.

Consider the overall attitude toward innovation and technology in your institution. How open are staff members to new ideas and approaches? Is there a culture of continuous learning and professional development?

Finally, reflect on the specific needs and challenges of your student population. Are there achievement gaps that need to be addressed? Do you have students with special educational needs? Are there particular subject areas where students consistently struggle?

Exercise: Conducting a Comprehensive Educational Environment Assessment

Objective: To gain a clear, data-driven understanding of your current educational environment.

Materials needed:

- survey creation tool (e.g., Google Forms or SurveyMonkey)

- spreadsheet software for data analysis

- access to school performance data

Steps

1. Create separate surveys for staff, students, and parents. Each survey should cover

o   technology access and usage

o   comfort level with various technologies

o   attitudes toward AI and technology in education

o   perceived challenges and needs in the current educational environment

2. Distribute the surveys and allow 1–2 weeks for responses.

3. While waiting for survey responses, gather quantitative data on

o   current technology infrastructure (internet speeds, number and types of devices, etc.)

o   student performance metrics (test scores, attendance rates, etc.)

o   teacher performance metrics (if available)

4. Once survey responses are in, analyze the data. Look for

o   patterns in technology usage and comfort levels

o   common concerns or excitement about AI integration

o   discrepancies between different stakeholder groups

5. Conduct follow-up focus groups or interviews to delve deeper into key findings from the surveys.

6. Create a comprehensive report that includes

o   quantitative data on technology infrastructure and performance metrics

o   qualitative data from surveys and focus groups

o   SWOT analysis (strengths, weaknesses, opportunities, and threats) based on your findings

7.   Present this report to key stakeholders and use it as a foundation for your AI integration planning.

This exercise will provide you with a comprehensive understanding of your current educational environment, serving as a crucial first step in your embodied AI integration journey.

Identifying Needs and Goals

With a clear understanding of your current environment, the next step is to identify your specific needs and set clear goals for embodied AI integration. This process will help ensure that your AI initiatives are purposeful and aligned with your overall educational objectives.

Begin by reflecting on your current teaching practices that already incorporate embodied, hands-on, experiential learning. What activities or methods have you found most effective in engaging students' minds and bodies simultaneously? Consider how these successful approaches align with your overall educational philosophy.

Next, identify areas where students consistently struggle to grasp concepts, particularly those that are abstract or historically challenging to teach. How might AI enhance or transform these difficult topics into more tangible, interactive experiences?

Now, articulate a clear vision for AI in your educational environment. How could AI amplify and extend the embodied learning experiences you're already creating? For example, if you're using physical manipulatives to teach mathematical concepts, how might AI-powered augmented reality enhance this approach? If you're conducting hands-on science experiments, how could AI simulations allow students to explore scenarios that aren't possible in a typical classroom setting?

Consider specific subjects or topics where you'd like to implement AI-enhanced learning. Perhaps you've always wanted to make historical events more vivid for your students or to help them visualize complex biological processes. How could AI help bring these ideas to life in a way that engages multiple senses and allows for active, embodied exploration?

As you develop this vision, ask yourself

- How do you envision AI enhancing your teaching and learning processes while staying true to your commitment to hands-on, experiential learning?

- What does success look like in terms of AI integration? How will you know if the AI-enhanced experiences are truly improving student understanding and engagement?

- How does this vision of AI-enhanced embodied learning align with and extend your overall educational philosophy?

The goal is not to replace your existing successful practices but to amplify and extend them, creating even more powerful embodied learning experiences for your students.

Based on your assessment, identify the key challenges that AI could help address. Are there areas where student engagement is low? Are there administrative tasks that are taking up too much of teachers' time? Are there subjects or concepts that students consistently find difficult?

Translate your vision and challenges into specific, measurable goals. For each goal, identify the AI capabilities you'll need to achieve it. Ensure that your goals address the needs of all stakeholders—students, teachers, administrators, and parents.

Exercise: AI Integration Vision and Goal-Setting Workshop

Objective: To create a shared, inclusive vision for AI integration and set specific, measurable goals.

Materials needed:

- digital collaboration platform (e.g., Microsoft Teams, Zoom, or Google Meet) with whiteboard and breakout room capabilities

- shared document for real-time collaboration (e.g., Google Docs)

- AI-powered transcription and summarization tool (e.g., Otter.ai)

- copy of your educational environment assessment report

Preworkshop preparation:

1. Research existing AI implementation solutions in education through established resources like the UNESCO AI in Education Clearinghouse, ISTE's AI in Education Network, and the European Schoolnet's AI implementation guidelines. Focus on documented case studies from diverse contexts— from large urban districts to small rural schools. Pay particular attention to institutions similar to yours in size, resources, and student demographics. As you review these examples, document specific strategies that align with your institution's goals and constraints.

2. Arrange for your IT professional to give a short presentation on current AI capabilities and upcoming plans in your institution.

3. Prepare a brief explanation of SMART goals (specific, measurable, achievable, relevant, and time-bound) and STEM (science, technology, engineering, and mathematics) for participants who may be unfamiliar.

Steps

1. Set up a hybrid meeting, allowing for both in-person and remote participation. Use an AI-powered transcription tool to record and summarize the session for those unable to attend.

2. Begin with brief presentations:

    o key findings from your educational environment assessment

    o overview of successful AI implementations in other institutions

    o current AI capabilities and future plans for your institution

3. Conduct a visioning exercise:

    o Ask participants to imagine their ideal embodied AI-enhanced learning environment five years from now.

    o Have them share their visions in the digital whiteboard or collaborative document.

    o Create a visual map of key themes using Miro or MindMeister. Place "Embodied AI-Enhanced Learning" at the center, then branch out with the main themes (Learning, Teaching, Administration, and Community). Use colors and icons to show relationships and priorities. Display the completed map prominently as your shared vision reference.

4. Based on the shared visions, use AI-powered language processing to draft a concise vision statement. Refine it collaboratively.

5. Conduct a challenge identification exercise:

    o Have participants submit their top three AI-addressable challenges via a digital form.

    o Use AI to cluster similar challenges and identify the top 5–7 based on frequency and impact.

6. For each prioritized challenge, use breakout rooms (virtual and physical) to brainstorm potential AI solutions. Consider

different types of AI (e.g., natural language processing, computer vision, machine learning).

7. Reconvene and translate the top challenges and potential solutions into SMART goals. For example: "Increase student engagement in STEM subjects by 30% within one year through the implementation of AI-powered interactive simulations."

8. For each goal, collaboratively identify

    o specific AI capabilities needed

    o potential barriers to achievement

    o key stakeholders who need to be involved

    o metrics for measuring success

9. Conclude the workshop by reviewing the vision statement and goals. Use a digital polling tool to ensure broad agreement and excitement about the direction.

10. Use an AI tool to compile and organize all the information generated during the workshop into a structured report, including a proposed timeline and list of needs.

Post-workshop actions:

1. Share the AI-generated report with all participants and relevant stakeholders.

2. Set up a digital platform (e.g., Slack channel) for ongoing discussion and idea-sharing about AI integration.

3. Assign the following tasks to participants, to be completed within a week:

    o Identify one current teaching practice that could be enhanced by AI.

- o Suggest one AI tool or application they'd like to learn more about.

- o Propose one way to make AI integration more inclusive in their area.

4. Use an AI-powered project management tool (e.g., Trello with AI capabilities) to organize and track the progress of these ideas and tasks.

This exercise will help create a shared vision and set of goals for AI integration, ensuring buy-in from various stakeholders and providing a clear direction for your efforts. Note: The specific tools suggested are examples only—use whatever methods work best for your team to maintain momentum and engagement. The goal is building a shared vision, not mastering particular technologies.

Building a Supportive School Culture

The success of your embodied AI integration efforts will depend greatly on the culture of your school or institution. A supportive culture that embraces innovation and values continuous enactive learning is essential.

Foster open communication by creating channels for dialogue about AI integration. Invest in ongoing professional development related to embodied AI in education. Recognize and celebrate successes in AI implementation, no matter how small. School leaders should model enthusiasm for AI integration. Create a safe space for teachers to experiment with AI tools. Proactively address common fears about AI in education.

Exercise: An Embodied AI Integration Culture-Building Program

Objective: To create a school culture that is open to and supportive of Embodied AI integration, involving all stakeholders in the process.

Materials needed:

- digital platforms for communication and collaboration (e.g., Microsoft Teams, Slack, or Padlet)

- budget for professional development and recognition programs

- AI tools for experimentation (e.g., Teachable Machine, AIY Projects, Machine Learning for Kids)

Steps

1. **Establish an "Embodied AI in Education" communication channel:**

   - Set up a dedicated channel on your chosen digital platform.

   - Post regular updates, including success stories like

     - a middle school math teacher using AI-powered gesture recognition to teach geometry concepts

     - an elementary school using AI chatbots to create interactive storytelling experiences

   - Encourage questions and discussions from teachers, students, and parents.

2. **Develop an AI literacy program for staff, students, and parents:**

   - Create a series of workshops covering AI basics and applications in education.

- o Make these workshops interactive, for example

    - ■ Use Teachable Machine to create a simple image recognition model

    - ■ Develop a chatbot using Dialogflow to answer common school-related questions

- o Offer incentives for participation, such as professional development credits for teachers and extra credit for students.

3. **Implement an "AI Innovation Challenge" for teachers and students:**

    - o Invite participants to propose ideas for AI integration in classrooms.

    - o Successful past projects include

        - ■ a high school biology class using AI to analyze local ecosystem data

        - ■ a group of elementary students creating an AI-powered recycling sorter

    - o Provide resources and support for implementation.

    - o Showcase results at a school-wide AI fair.

4. **Create an "AI Lab" for experimentation:**

    - o Designate a physical and virtual space for AI exploration.

    - o Stock the lab with tools like

        - ■ Cozmo educational robots for coding and AI concepts

- virtual reality (VR) headsets for immersive learning experiences

- AI-powered language learning software

○ Schedule regular "open lab" times for teachers, students, and parents.

5. **Establish an "AI Champion" program:**

   ○ Identify enthusiastic teachers, students, and parents.

   ○ Provide advanced training through online courses (e.g., Elements of AI or AI for Everyone).

   ○ Task champions with mentoring others and leading integration efforts.

6. **Host regular "AI in Education" events:**

   ○ Organize monthly showcases of AI integration efforts.

   ○ Invite speakers like local tech entrepreneurs or AI researchers.

   ○ Include student-led demonstrations of AI projects.

7. **Address fears and concerns proactively:**

   ○ Host open forums for all stakeholders to voice concerns.

   ○ Provide clear information on AI use, addressing issues like

      - data privacy in AI-powered learning platforms

      - the role of AI in assessment and grading

   ○ Emphasize AI as a tool to augment, not replace, human teaching.

8. **Model AI use at all levels:**

   o School leaders use AI tools in administrative tasks.

   o Teachers incorporate AI in lesson planning and delivery.

   o Students use AI in projects and presentations.

   o Share both successes (e.g., improved engagement in STEM subjects) and challenges (e.g., technical glitches in AI implementations) to normalize the learning process.

9. **Establish feedback mechanisms:**

   o Use AI-powered survey tools to regularly gather feedback from all stakeholders.

   o Implement changes based on feedback, such as

      ■ adjusting the pace of AI integration based on teacher comfort levels

      ■ expanding AI tools based on student interest and engagement

10. **Continuous learning and adaptation:**

   o Regularly update your AI integration approach based on

      ■ new technological developments (e.g., advances in natural language processing)

      ■ emerging best practices in AI education

      ■ feedback from your school community

This comprehensive program will help create a school culture that is not just accepting of AI integration but also actively enthusiastic about its potential to enhance teaching and learning.

Addressing Ethical Considerations

As we integrate AI into education, it's crucial to consider the ethical implications of these technologies. Key areas to address include data privacy and security, algorithmic bias, transparency and explainability, equity and accessibility, human oversight and control, as well as digital citizenship and AI literacy.

Exercise: Developing an AI Ethics Framework

Objective: To create a comprehensive ethical framework for AI use in your educational institution and establish necessary committees for ongoing oversight.

Materials needed:

- existing school policies on technology use and data privacy

- resources on AI ethics in education (e.g., UNESCO's *AI in Education: Guidance for Policy-Makers*)

- collaborative document editing tool (e.g., Google Docs)

- video conferencing platform for hybrid meetings (e.g., Zoom)

Pre-exercise reading:

- *The Ethics of Artificial Intelligence in Education* by Wayne Holmes et al.

Steps

1. **Form core committees:** In your initial meeting, highlight the need for various committees and ask for volunteers:

    o   AI Ethics Committee

    o   AI Implementation Committee

    o   AI Curriculum Integration Committee

    o   AI Professional Development Committee

    o   AI Community Engagement Committee

2. **Conduct an AI ethics workshop:**

    o   Format: A hybrid webinar series with interactive elements

    o   Organizer: AI Ethics Committee, potentially in collaboration with a local university's ethics department

    o   Content:

        ▪   key ethical issues in AI and education

        ▪   case studies and interactive scenarios

        ▪   guest speakers from other schools successfully implementing ethical AI frameworks

    o   Participation: Make it part of mandatory professional development, with online modules and in-person discussion sessions.

3. **Review existing policies:**

    o   Task the AI Ethics Committee with examining current policies.

    ○   Use AI-powered document analysis tools to identify gaps in existing policies.

4. **Develop ethical guidelines:**

    ○   Create collaborative online workspaces for each key area (data privacy, algorithmic bias, etc.).

    ○   Use real-world examples, such as

        ■   Data privacy: How to handle AI-generated student performance predictions

        ■   Algorithmic bias: Ensuring fairness in AI-powered admissions or scholarship algorithms

5. **Create an AI decision-making framework:**

    ○   Develop an interactive flowchart tool for evaluating new AI implementations.

    ○   Include questions like: "How does this AI tool align with our school's values and mission?"

6. **Establish monitoring and auditing processes:**

    ○   Implement an AI ethics dashboard for real-time monitoring of AI systems

    ○   Schedule quarterly audits, alternating between internal and external reviewers.

7. **Develop an AI literacy curriculum:**

    ○   Collaborate with the AI Curriculum Integration Committee.

    ○   Reference existing programs like "AI for K-12" by AI4K12.org

8. **Create a transparent communication plan:**

   o Work with the AI Community Engagement Committee.

   o Develop a dedicated AI ethics section on the school website.

   o Create an "AI in Our School" newsletter for regular updates.

9. **Establish an ethics review process:**

   o Implement a stage-gate process for new AI tools, with an ethics review at each stage.

   o Create an online submission and review platform for proposed AI implementations.

10. **Plan for ongoing review and revision:**

    o Schedule annual AI ethics symposiums to discuss emerging issues and update policies.

    o Join networks like the Global AI Ethics Consortium for Education to stay informed of best practices.

Additional resources:

- "AI Ethics Guide" by the International Society for Technology in Education (ISTE)

- "Artificial Intelligence in Education for Teachers" MOOC on Coursera

- Institute for Ethical AI in Education website

This exercise will help you create a robust ethical framework for AI use in your school, ensuring that your AI integration efforts are not just effective, but also responsible and trustworthy.

Budgeting and Resource Allocation

Effective AI integration requires careful budgeting and strategic allocation of resources. This includes conducting a cost–benefit analysis, identifying funding sources, investing in infrastructure, allocating resources for training, planning for ongoing support and maintenance, and creating a contingency fund.

Exercise: AI Integration Budget Planning Workshop

Objective: To create a comprehensive budget plan for AI integration.

Materials needed:

- current school budget

- cost estimates for potential AI tools and infrastructure upgrades

- spreadsheet software

Steps

1. **Assemble a budget planning team:**

   o Include representatives from administration, IT, and teaching staff.

   o Consider involving a financial advisor with experience in educational technology.

2. **Review the current budget:**

   o Analyze your current technology and professional development budgets.

     o   Identify areas where funds could potentially be reallocated to AI initiatives.

3. **Conduct a needs assessment:**

     o   Based on your earlier goal-setting exercise, list all the AI tools and resources you'll need.

     o   Include both immediate needs and projected future requirements.

4. **Research costs:**

     o   Obtain quotes for all identified AI tools and resources.

     o   Don't forget to include costs for training, ongoing support, and potential infrastructure upgrades.

5. **Perform a cost–benefit analysis:**

     o   For each major AI initiative, estimate both the costs and the potential benefits (both quantitative and qualitative).

     o   Use this analysis to prioritize your AI investments.

6. **Identify funding sources:**

     o   Explore various funding options, including reallocation of existing funds, grants, partnerships with tech companies, and fundraising initiatives.

     o   Create a plan for pursuing each potential funding source.

7. **Create a multiyear budget:**

     o   Develop a 3 to 5-year budget plan for AI integration.

- Include both one-time costs (like initial hardware purchases) and ongoing costs (like software subscriptions and maintenance).

8. **Plan for professional development:**

    - Allocate a significant portion of your budget to staff training and development.

    - Include costs for both initial training and ongoing learning opportunities.

9. **Build in flexibility:**

    - Create a contingency fund (aim for 10%–15% of your total AI budget) for unexpected costs or opportunities.

    - Plan for regular budget reviews and adjustments as your AI integration progresses by aligning with the regular cadence of other budget planning processes.

10. **Develop a return on investment tracking system:**

    - Create a system for tracking the impact of your AI investments.

    - Include both quantitative metrics (like improved test scores) and qualitative measures (like increased student engagement).

11. **Create a budget presentation:**

    - Develop a clear, compelling presentation of your AI integration budget.

    - Be prepared to explain and justify each major expense.

This exercise will help you create a comprehensive, realistic budget for your AI integration efforts, ensuring that you have the necessary resources to support your initiatives over the long term.

Creating an Embodied AI Integration Timeline

A well-structured timeline is crucial for successful embodied AI integration. It helps ensure that you're moving forward at an appropriate pace, allows you to set realistic expectations, and helps you coordinate various aspects of the integration process.

Exercise: Embodied AI Integration Road Map Creation

Objective: To create a realistic, easy-to-follow timeline for embodied AI integration in your school using familiar planning models.

Materials needed:

- spreadsheet software (e.g., Microsoft Excel or Google Sheets)

- results from previous exercises (goals, budget, etc.)

- academic calendar

- 12 Week Year planning template (optional)

Example resources:

- For a sample technology integration plan, explore the Common Sense Education website, which provides a variety of technology integration resources and frameworks, including educational technology (edtech) reviews and digital citizenship curricula. You can also find comprehensive case studies and lesson plans on technology integration by visiting Edutopia.

- To see an example of a 12 Week Year template adapted for education, check out resources from Teacher Habits, where time-management strategies and templates are tailored for educators. Additionally, Cult of Pedagogy offers productivity strategies and professional development tips that can help educators implement a structured approach similar to the 12 Week Year method.

- For insights on long-term strategic planning in education, visit the Association for Supervision and Curriculum Development website, which provides strategic planning resources focused on curriculum development and school improvement. You can also explore strategic planning tools and templates on Education World, which offers practical guides for school leaders.

Steps

1. **Assemble a timeline planning team:**

   o Include representatives from administration, IT, and teaching staff.

2. **Choose a planning model:**

   o Decide between an academic year model, a 12 Week Year model, or a 5-4-3-2-1 year model.

   o For this exercise, we'll use the 5-4-3-2-1 year model for simplicity.

3. **Set up your spreadsheet:**

   o Create columns for each period: 5 Year, 4 Year, 3 Year, 2 Year, 1 Year.

   o Add rows for different aspects of AI integration: Infrastructure, Training, Curriculum Integration, and Evaluation.

4. **Review and prioritize your AI integration goals:**

   o Place each goal in the appropriate time frame column.

5. **Break down near-term goals:**

   o For goals in the 1-2 year columns, break them down into specific tasks.

6. **Align with academic calendar:**

   o Use color coding to indicate how tasks align with academic terms or breaks.

7. **Assign responsibilities:**

   o Add a column to indicate who is responsible for each task or goal.

8. **Set milestones:**

   o Highlight key milestones in your spreadsheet.

9. **Build in review points:**

   o Add quarterly review points to your timeline.

Example 5-4-3-2-1 Year Plan

- 5 year:

  o Full AI integration across all subjects and grade levels

  o AI-driven personalized learning for every student

- 4 year:

  o AI-enhanced STEM curriculum fully implemented

  o All staff trained in advanced AI integration techniques

- 3 year:

  o Pilot AI-driven assessment tools.

- ○ Implement AI ethics curriculum.

- 2 year:

  - ○ Train all staff in basic AI integration.

  - ○ Implement AI in core subjects (math, science, and language arts)

- 1 year:

  - ○ Assess current technology infrastructure.

  - ○ Pilot AI in one grade level or subject.

  - ○ Develop an embodied AI integration plan.

This exercise will help you create a comprehensive, realistic timeline for your embodied AI integration efforts. Remember, this timeline should be a living document, regularly reviewed and updated as your integration progresses and you learn from your experiences.

By thoroughly addressing these aspects of preparation—assessing your environment, identifying needs and goals, building a supportive culture, addressing ethical considerations, budgeting effectively, and creating a realistic timeline—you'll be well-positioned to begin your journey of embodying AI in your educational practice. The key is to approach embodied AI integration as an organic extension of your teaching and learning processes.

Consider how embodied AI can be woven into the fabric of daily educational experiences:

- How can embodied AI enhance hands-on learning activities?

- In what ways can embodied AI support students' physical engagement with concepts?

- How might embodied AI facilitate more intuitive, natural interactions with educational content?

The goal is to make AI an invisible yet integral part of the learning environment, seamlessly blending with traditional teaching methods to create rich, multisensory educational experiences. By doing so, AI becomes a natural extension of the learning process, as familiar and essential as a pencil or a textbook.

Remember, truly embodied AI integration means that students and teachers alike don't just use AI—they experience it, interact with it, and enactively learn through it in ways that engage their minds and bodies holistically. This approach ensures that AI becomes part of who they are as learners and educators.

Let's recap the key points from this section:

1. **Assessment is crucial:** Understanding your current educational environment is the foundation for successful embodied AI integration.

2. **Clear goals drive success:** Identifying specific, measurable goals will guide your embodied AI integration efforts.

3. **Culture matters:** Building a supportive school culture is essential for successful embodied AI adoption.

4. **Ethics can't be an afterthought:** Addressing ethical considerations from the start ensures responsible embodied AI use.

5. **Budgeting is key:** Careful resource allocation supports sustainable embodied AI integration.

6. **Timelines provide structure:** A well-planned timeline keeps your embodied AI integration efforts on track.

To simplify the journey of embodying AI in your educational practice, let's distill the process into six essential steps: assess your environment, set clear goals, foster a supportive culture, address ethical considerations, allocate resources effectively, and create a realistic timeline. By focusing on these key areas, you can navigate the complexities of embodied AI integration with confidence.

This is an iterative process. As you progress, be prepared to learn, adjust, and evolve your approach. Embrace the journey of discovery, knowing that each small advancement brings you closer to a learning environment where AI seamlessly enhances embodied, experiential education. With this roadmap in hand, you're well-equipped to begin transforming your educational practice, creating rich, multisensory experiences that engage students' minds and bodies holistically. The future of education is about experiencing AI, interacting with it, and learning through it in ways that make technology an invisible yet integral part of the enactive learning process.

Chapter 2:

Developing Embodied AI Literacy

In our rapidly evolving educational landscape, embodied AI literacy has become as crucial as traditional forms of literacy. This chapter explores how to develop embodied AI literacy across various stakeholder groups, providing targeted strategies and practical exercises for each.

For Administrators: Leading the AI Revolution

As the captains of our educational institutions, administrators must chart the course for AI integration. Your understanding of AI will shape the technological landscape of your schools.

Key focus areas:

1. Embodied AI fundamentals

2. Strategic embodied AI implementation

3. Ethical considerations

4. Resource management

Exercise: AI Readiness Assessment

Objective: Evaluate your institution's readiness for embodied AI integration.

Steps:

1. Create a survey covering

- current technological infrastructure

  - staff AI knowledge and attitudes

  - potential areas for embodied AI implementation

2. Distribute the survey to staff members.

3. Analyze results to identify strengths and gaps.

4. Develop an action plan based on the findings.

The AI readiness assessment shouldn't be just another survey. One district transformed its traditional administrative meetings by starting each session with hands-on AI experiences. At one memorable meeting, administrators arrived to find VR headsets at their seats. Instead of beginning with budget discussions, they spent 20 minutes experiencing a virtual classroom where AI adapted in real time to student responses.

The subsequent discussion about AI implementation was markedly different—more engaged, practical, and grounded in personal experience. Another month, they tested an AI-powered translation tool by conversing with parents from different language backgrounds. These experiential starts to meetings shifted the conversation from theoretical to practical, from "what if" to "how can we."

Your leadership sets the tone for AI adoption. Stay curious, remain open to learning, and model the embodied AI literacy you wish to see in your staff and students.

For Teachers: AI in the Classroom

As educators, you're on the front lines of the AI revolution in education. Your ability to leverage AI tools will directly impact student learning experiences.

Let's explore embodied AI integration through a typical school day:

1. Morning: Use AI for attendance and scheduling optimization

2. Lesson time: Incorporate AI-powered adaptive learning platforms

3. Assessment: Utilize AI for real-time formative assessments

4. After school: Analyze student data with AI to inform future lessons

Exercise: AI-Enhanced Lesson Plan

Objective: Create a lesson plan that meaningfully incorporates AI.

Steps:

1. Choose a topic from your curriculum.

2. Identify an AI tool that could enhance learning (e.g., a virtual reality app for history or a language processing tool for writing).

3. Design a lesson plan integrating the AI tool.

4. Include pre and post-activity assessments to measure the AI tool's impact.

5. Implement the lesson and reflect on the outcomes.

Remember, AI is just one tool to augment your teaching. Your expertise and human touch remain irreplaceable in the learning process.

For Students: Growing Up With AI

Dear students, you're growing up in a world where AI is becoming ubiquitous. Understanding AI is more about keeping up with technology—it's about shaping your future.

Imagine a day in your life in 2030:

- Your AI alarm wakes you at the optimal time based on your sleep patterns.

- Your personalized AI tutor helps you prepare for exams.

- You collaborate with classmates globally using AI-powered translation tools.

- Your afternoon soccer practice uses AI analysis to improve your technique.

This is the exciting world you are stepping into. Let's prepare you for it.

Exercise: AI Detective Challenge

Objective: Identify AI in your daily life and understand its impact.

Steps:

1. Keep a diary for a week, noting every interaction with AI (Hint: It's in more places than you think!).

2. For each AI interaction, answer

    o What does this AI do?

    o How does it make my life easier?

    o What data might it be collecting about me?

3. At the end of the week, reflect on

    o Which AI surprised you most?

    o Are there areas of your life where AI could be helpful but isn't present?

○   What concerns do you have about AI in your life?

Remember, you're AI's future creators and regulators. Stay curious, ask questions, and never stop learning.

For Parents and Community: Understanding the AI in Your Child's Backpack

As parents and community members, you're already engaging with AI in many aspects of daily life—from smart home devices to navigation apps to entertainment platforms. This familiarity provides an excellent foundation for understanding and supporting AI in education. Your active participation helps create a bridge between home and school technology experiences, enriching your child's learning journey.

Let's start by exploring the AI tools you're already using:

1.   What apps and devices in your home use AI to make life easier?

2.   How do you and your children interact with these tools?

3.   Which of these experiences might enhance learning?

Family Technology Inventory Exercise

- List the smart devices and apps your family uses daily.

- Identify which ones could support learning.

- Share your findings with your child's teachers.

- Connect with other parents to exchange ideas about positive AI experiences.

Many of your everyday AI experiences can spark meaningful conversations about technology in education. Your insights and questions are valuable—share them through your school's AI committee or parent advisory group to help shape thoughtful implementation.

Exercise: Family AI Night

Objective: Explore AI as a family in a fun, interactive way, celebrating each family member's interests and expertise.

Steps:

1. **Family tech show-and-tell:**

    - Each family member shares an AI tool they're excited to learn about.

    - Kids teach parents their favorite AI-powered games.

    - Parents demonstrate AI tools they use at work.

    - Grandparents might share an interest in AI health or home assistants.

2. **Create a learning partners system:**

    - Match family members based on their interests and knowledge.

        - Example: Teen teaches parent TikTok AI features while parent shows AI work tools.

    - Younger children might pair with older siblings to explore educational AI games.

3. **Choose one new AI tool to explore together:**

    - Each family member takes turns being the "expert" or guide.

○ Document what you discover through photos or short videos.

○ Share amusing moments of role reversal when kids become the teachers.

4. **Create a family learning wish list:**

○ List AI tools each family member wants to learn.

○ Note who in the family might be the best teacher for each tool.

○ Plan future family tech nights around these interests.

Learning about AI can be a two-way street—sometimes, children will be the experts, and sometimes, parents will lead the way. Embrace the opportunity to learn from each other!

For Innovators: Pushing the Boundaries of AI in Education

Innovation in educational AI comes from more than just tech companies or research labs—it emerges from diverse experiences and perspectives. Whether you're a parent who's discovered a better way to teach math through AI games, a small business owner who's developed clever AI workflows, a teacher who's created innovative classroom tools, or a student who sees possibilities others might miss, your insights can shape the future of embodying educational AI.

Our innovators come from everywhere:

• parents who've developed creative AI solutions for homework help

• small business owners applying their AI automation experience to education

- teachers creating classroom-tested AI tools

- healthcare workers bringing wellness-tracking insights to schools

- artists integrating AI into creative education

- gamers identifying engaging learning mechanics

- students seeing gaps that current solutions miss

Key Considerations for All Innovators

1. **Ground-up design:**

    o What real-world problems have you solved with AI?

    o How might your solution help others learn?

    o What unique perspective does your background bring?

2. **Collaborative approach:**

    o Connect with educators to understand classroom needs

    o Partner with students for real-world testing

    o Share insights with other innovators from different fields

3. **Practical implementation:**

    o Consider how your solution fits into daily life

    o Build on tools people already use

    o Make it accessible for various skill levels

4. **Community integration:**

   ○ How can local businesses support educational AI?

   ○ What role can community spaces play?

   ○ How might families contribute to development?

Exercise: AI Education Hackathon

Objective: Develop AI-powered educational solutions through sustained student-led projects, connecting with existing STEM programs and real-world applications.

Steps:

1. **Launch year-round innovation tracks:**

   ○ Robotics club AI enhancement projects

   ○ Science fair AI category

   ○ Student tech support team AI solutions

   ○ Cross-disciplinary projects (art + AI or sports + AI)

2. **Build mixed experience teams:**

   ○ student innovators from different grade levels

   ○ teacher mentors

   ○ industry partners (local tech companies, parents in tech)

   ○ community organizations

   ○ current AI tool users sharing practical insights

3. **Real-world problem-solving:**

    ○ Identify challenges in your school or community.

    ○ Connect with local businesses to understand their AI needs.

    ○ Partner with other schools for a wider perspective.

    ○ Build on existing successful programs.

4. **Ongoing development cycle:**

    ○ weekly team meetings during lunch or after school

    ○ monthly progress showcases

    ○ integration with science fairs and tech competitions

    ○ regular testing in real classroom settings

5. **Student leadership opportunities:**

    ○ project management roles

    ○ mentoring younger students

    ○ presenting at educational conferences

    ○ contributing to school AI policy

6. **Showcase and scale:**

    ○ annual AI innovation fair

    ○ student-led workshops for the community

    ○ documentation for other schools to replicate

    ○ online platform to share progress

Success is realized through creating sustained engagement where students drive innovation while building real-world skills and connections.

For Small Businesses: Riding the AI Wave

In the educational technology landscape, small businesses have a unique advantage: agility. Your ability to quickly adapt and innovate with AI can set you apart in a competitive market.

AI opportunities for edtech SMEs:

1. Personalized learning platforms

2. AI-powered tutoring systems

3. Educational chatbots

4. Learning analytics tools

5. AI-enhanced content creation

Exercise: AI Business Model Canvas

Objective: Identify how embodied AI can enhance your business model.

Steps:

1. Create a traditional business model canvas for your company.

2. For each section, brainstorm

   o How could AI enhance this?

   o What new opportunities does AI create here?

3. Identify the top three AI opportunities for your business.

4. For each opportunity, outline

   ○ potential benefits

   ○ required resources

   ○ possible challenges

5. Create an action plan to explore your top AI opportunity.

Remember, AI is a tool to enhance your unique value proposition, not a replacement for it. Focus on how embodying AI can help you serve your educational customers better.

Ongoing Embodied AI Education Strategies: Learning Through Movement and Connection

The transformation of one school's AI literacy program began with a simple observation. A physics teacher noticed during robotics club sessions that students naturally moved their bodies to work out robot movement sequences before programming them. Students would stand, gesture, and physically map out the paths they wanted their robots to take, translating bodily understanding into code.

This observation sparked the development of their Move-Think-Code program. Rather than traditional AI training sessions with participants seated at computers, the school created learning spaces that engaged the whole body. The program evolved organically from those first robotics club sessions.

The breakthrough moment came during the school's first intergenerational AI learning day. Grandparents learned alongside kindergarteners, using movement to understand AI concepts. One grandmother, who had initially expressed strong skepticism about technology, discovered she could understand neural networks by participating in a human chain of "neurons," passing messages through a living network. Within months, she became one of the program's most passionate advocates, leading sessions for other seniors in the community.

The program expanded naturally across disciplines. The physical education department incorporated AI concepts into games that demonstrated machine learning principles through movement. Dance classes explored how AI analyzes motion, with students teaching motion-capture systems new dance moves. The school counseling team adopted movement-based activities to help students explore their relationship with AI in their daily lives.

Most significantly, this embodied approach dismantled traditional barriers to AI understanding. Adults who had labeled themselves "too old" for technology found themselves naturally engaging when concepts came alive through movement and play. Students who struggled with traditional learning methods discovered new paths to understanding when they could physically experience the concepts.

The program continues to evolve, guided by three principles:

- learn through doing

- teach through movement

- connect across generations

The impact extends beyond an improved understanding of AI concepts to stronger community bonds, increased empathy, and more inclusive technology education. The school's upcoming AI in Motion workshops will bring families together to learn about AI through dance, sports, and interactive games, while robotics students design movement-based learning experiences for younger children.

This approach demonstrates how embodied AI literacy transcends traditional technical training. By engaging the whole person—body, mind, and community connections—learning becomes more accessible, meaningful, and lasting.

Exercise: Personal AI Learning Plan

Objective: Create a personalized roadmap for ongoing embodied AI literacy development.

Steps:

1. Assess your current AI literacy level.

2. Identify 3 AI skills you want to develop.

3. For each skill, list

    ○ learning resources (courses, books, and workshops)

    ○ practice opportunities

    ○ assessment methods

4. Set specific, measurable goals for each skill.

5. Create a timeline for achieving these goals.

6. Identify an accountability partner.

7. Schedule regular check-ins to review progress.

Remember, embodied AI literacy is a journey toward your greatest potential. Embrace a growth mindset and commit to lifelong learning in this rapidly evolving field.

By tailoring embodied AI literacy development to each stakeholder group and providing practical exercises, we can create an ecosystem where embodied AI enhances human intelligence in education. As we navigate this AI revolution, let's strive to use these powerful tools to create more engaging, effective, and equitable learning experiences for all.

Chapter 3:

Choosing the Right Embodied AI

Tools

The journey of integrating embodied AI in classroom practice transcends simple technology adoption. For many educators, the initial steps can feel overwhelming. Remember: You're not meant to walk this path alone. Whether you're partnering with a colleague down the hall, joining a cross-district study group, or connecting with online communities of practice, the key lies in finding your support network. As one teacher noted, "What seemed impossible alone became exciting when we explored it together."

Integrating Embodied AI in Lesson Planning

Traditional lesson planning often pulls teachers away from the hands-on, interactive aspects of preparation that benefit students most. Through thoughtful integration of embodied AI in your planning process, you can return to the physical and creative elements that make teaching come alive.

One middle school teaching team discovered this transformation gradually. They began by observing how students naturally moved and interacted during successful lessons. These observations informed how they integrated embodied AI into their planning—not as a separate technology layer, but as a natural extension of their teaching instincts. Their journey offers valuable insights for others beginning this process.

Building Your Support Network

Before diving into tools and techniques, consider

- Who might share this journey with you?

- Which colleagues naturally complement your strengths?

- What expertise already exists in your school community?

- How might you support each other's growth?

The power of collaborative exploration became evident in one district where teachers formed what they called "AI exploration circles"— small groups meeting regularly to share discoveries, challenges, and successes. These circles provided both practical support and emotional encouragement during the integration process.

Exercise: Collaborative Planning Evolution

Objective: Transform your planning process while building supportive partnerships.

Note: These exercises begin as separate steps to build confidence and understanding. Over time, you'll find them naturally merging into a seamless practice with embodied AI. As one teacher noted, "What started as distinct activities gradually became our natural way of working."

Preparation phase: Start by gathering with your planning partners to explore fundamental questions. One successful teaching team began by spending a full afternoon sharing their experiences and hopes:

Deep reflection questions:

- What aspects of planning bring you joy and energy?

- Where do you feel most constrained by routine tasks?

- How do you naturally incorporate movement and physical engagement?

- What support would help you take creative risks?

Consider documenting these conversations. A high school English department created what they called their "Journey Journal," recording insights and questions that later proved invaluable in guiding their integration process.

Implementation Journey

Week 1: Exploration and Discovery

Morning reflection: Begin each day by considering your current practice through new lenses. One elementary team started their mornings 15 minutes early to observe and discuss:

- How do students move and interact during your best lessons?

- When do you see natural learning moments emerge?

- What patterns support deeper engagement?

- Where could embodied AI enhance these natural rhythms?

Their observations revealed unexpected patterns—students often demonstrated understanding through movement before they could verbalize concepts, an insight that transformed how they integrated embodied AI into their planning.

Afternoon integration: Use this time to collaborate deeply with your planning partners. One middle school team transformed their traditional planning period into what they called their "Innovation Workshop," where they

- explored which teaching moments could benefit from embodied AI support

- mapped how AI might help track and respond to natural learning patterns

- identified opportunities for deeper physical engagement

- shared exciting possibilities and concerns

Week 2: Embodied AI Tool Exploration

Rather than rushing to implement technology, take time to physically experience how embodied AI might enhance your teaching. A successful science department approached this by creating what they called "learning labs"—protected time and space for experimentation without pressure.

- **Day 1–2: Physical space mapping:** Begin with your planning partners by literally walking through your learning spaces. One team photographed and mapped their classrooms, noting

    o natural student movement patterns

    o informal collaboration spots

    o common traffic flows

    o physical barriers to learning

    o potential technology integration points

They discovered that understanding the physical space deeply informed their embodied AI implementation choices.

- **Day 3–5: Tool experimentation:** Remember, the goal toward mastery begins with comfortable exploration. A group of math teachers found success by

    o choosing one embodied AI tool that intrigued them

    o practicing with each other before trying with students

- recording what worked and what didn't

- celebrating small victories and learning from challenges

Their approach of "playful experimentation" helped reduce anxiety about technology integration.

- **Day 6–10: Collaborative creation:** This is where separate elements begin merging into natural practice. An elementary team discovered that by:

  - starting with their strongest teaching moments

  - gradually adding embodied AI support

  - documenting unexpected successes

  - supporting each other through challenges

They developed what they called "hybrid confidence"—the ability to move fluidly between traditional teaching practices while embodying AI-enhanced teaching methods.

Personalized Learning With Embodied AI

The power of personalization emerges when human insight meets embodied AI capabilities. A high school humanities department made a remarkable discovery: by using embodied AI to track and support natural learning patterns, they could create what they termed "responsive learning environments"—spaces that adapted to student needs in real time.

Exercise: Personalization Journey

Remember: Start with small steps that feel manageable. A successful middle school team began with just one class period, gradually expanding their use of embodied AI as their confidence grew.

Week 1: Natural Learning Observation

Morning explorations: Begin by gathering with colleagues to observe learning in its natural state. One effective approach came from a team that spent their first week simply watching and documenting

- different ways students physically express understanding

- variations in movement patterns during learning

- natural collaboration rhythms

- moments of spontaneous engagement

They created what they called "learning pattern maps"—visual representations of how students naturally moved and interacted during different types of activities.

Afternoon reflections: Use this time to deepen understanding with your support team. A successful elementary group scheduled daily "pattern talks" where they

- shared observations about physical learning styles

- discussed how different students demonstrated understanding

- identified patterns that embodied AI might help support

- planned ways to enhance natural learning rhythms

Rather than focusing immediately on technical setup, begin with understanding human patterns. A high school team transformed their approach by first creating what they called "learning journey maps" for each student.

Creating learning profiles: Work with colleagues to document

- natural learning preferences

- physical expression patterns

- social interaction styles

- environmental needs

One team discovered that by understanding these patterns deeply before implementing embodied AI, they could create more effective personalized learning experiences.

Project-Based Learning With Embodied AI

Project-based learning provides natural opportunities for embodied AI integration. A middle school STEM team discovered that by allowing embodied AI to support rather than direct project work, they created what they called "enhanced exploration spaces"—environments where technology amplified natural curiosity and creativity.

Deep Dive: Project Evolution

Consider how one successful teaching team approached their transformation:

Initial phase—Understanding natural patterns: They spent two weeks observing

- how students naturally approached problems

- when collaboration happened organically

- where physical movement enhanced learning

- what environmental factors supported creativity

Their observations led to what they called "project flow maps"—documenting how students naturally moved through different project phases. These maps later informed their embodied AI integration choices.

Exercise: Project Evolution Workshop

Foundation Building: Week 1—Physical Space Design

Morning observations: Begin by mapping your project space with colleagues. One art teacher's team spent their first week creating what they called a "movement heat map":

- tracking natural gathering points

- noting creative collaboration spaces

- identifying movement patterns

- observing energy flows

These observations revealed unexpected insights about how students naturally engage in project work.

Afternoon design sessions: Use these insights to plan embodied AI integration. A successful engineering program approached this by

- identifying natural workflow patterns

- planning technology support points

- designing flexible learning spaces

- creating what they called "AI enhancement zones"

Week 2: Integration Planning

Rather than implementing everything at once, focus on what one team called "natural enhancement points"—places where embodied AI could support existing patterns:

- **Monday and Tuesday—Pattern recognition:**

    o document successful project approaches

    o identify common challenges

    o map collaboration patterns

    o note physical learning preferences

- **Wednesday and Thursday—Support design:**

    o plan embodied AI integration points

    o design flexible support systems

    o create feedback mechanisms

    o develop adaptation strategies

- **Friday—Reflection and adjustment:**

    o review initial plans

    o share team insights

    o adjust approaches

    o plan next steps

Assessment With Embodied AI

Assessment transforms when we recognize and value physical demonstrations of learning. One humanities department revolutionized their approach by creating what they called "movement-aware rubrics"—assessment tools that incorporated embodied AI to capture and evaluate physical expressions of understanding.

Exercise: Assessment Evolution Journey

Begin by forming what one successful team called an "assessment reimagining circle"—a small group committed to exploring how embodied AI can enhance evaluation practices.

Creating holistic rubrics: Start with deep observation. One science department spent three weeks documenting

- physical demonstrations of understanding

- movement patterns that indicated learning

- collaborative knowledge-sharing

- spontaneous teaching moments between students

Their discoveries led to rich discussions about what learning looks like beyond traditional measures.

Example Rubric Transformation

Traditional physics assessment: "Student can explain Newton's Laws of Motion."

Evolved embodied AI assessment: "Student demonstrates understanding through

- physical modeling of force relationships

- real-time adaptation of demonstrations based on questions

- collaborative movement experiments

- creation of novel demonstrations

- spontaneous application to real-world scenarios"

The embodied AI system tracks and analyzes these physical demonstrations, providing insights about

- pattern recognition in student movements

- development of physical understanding over time

- variations in demonstration approaches

- unexpected learning moments

Week 1: Assessment Reimagining

Morning exploration: Gather with your assessment team to observe learning in action. One middle school team created what they called "learning journey maps":

- documenting physical expressions of understanding

- noting transitions in comprehension

- recording collaborative learning patterns

- identifying key assessment moments

Afternoon analysis: Use team time to

- share observation insights

- identify assessment opportunities

- plan embodied AI support points

- design new evaluation approaches

Classroom Management With Embodied AI

The transformation of classroom management comes through understanding how space, movement, and technology work together harmoniously. A middle school team discovered that by using embodied AI to support rather than control movement, they created what they called "living–learning spaces"—environments that adapted to and supported natural learning rhythms.

Exercise: Environment Evolution Workshop— Understanding Natural Patterns

Week 1: Deep Observation

Begin each day by observing different aspects of classroom flow. One successful team created what they called "energy maps":

Morning focus:

- peak engagement periods

- natural transition times

- movement patterns

- collaboration rhythms

Their observations revealed that student behavior often followed predictable patterns that embodied AI could help support.

Afternoon analysis: With your support team, document

- successful learning moments

- natural collaboration patterns

- transition challenges

- environmental influences

Week 2: Pattern Response Design

Use your observations to plan embodied AI integration:

- **Monday to Tuesday—Space planning:**

  - map movement flows

  - identify technology support points

  - plan flexible arrangements

  - design responsive zones

- **Wednesday to Thursday—System design:**

Create what one team called "responsive support structures":

  - natural transition cues

  - movement-friendly routines

  - flexible grouping patterns

  - adaptive space arrangements

- **Friday—Integration planning:**

  - review proposed changes

  - plan gradual implementation

  - design feedback systems

  - schedule adjustment points

One elementary team's transformation offers valuable insights. They began by

1. Creating movement baseline data

2. Identifying natural flow patterns

3. Planning supportive technology integration

4. Implementing gradual changes

Their "responsive classroom" approach led to

- improved student engagement

- reduced behavior issues

- more natural transitions

- enhanced learning focus

Balancing Traditional and Embodied AI Approaches

Integration success comes through enhancement, enactive learning experiences. A veteran teaching team discovered this truth through what they called their "harmony approach"—thoughtfully blending traditional wisdom with embodied AI support.

Exercise: Finding Your Teaching Harmony

Phase 1: Understanding Your Teaching Ecosystem

Week 1: Personal Practice

Mapping: Begin by documenting what one successful team called their "teaching signatures":

- natural teaching rhythms

- successful engagement strategies

- effective learning moments

- current technology use

Through this process, they discovered unique patterns that informed their embodied AI integration choices.

Week 2: Integration Exploration

With your support team, examine potential enhancement points:

- Where could embodied AI amplify existing strengths?

- Which teaching moments might benefit from technology support?

- How could natural teaching patterns be preserved and enhanced?

- What concerns need addressing?

One high school team created what they called "integration journey maps"—visual representations of how embodied AI could seamlessly enhance their teaching practice.

Phase 2: Thoughtful Implementation

Week 3: Gradual Integration

Start with what experienced teams call "natural entry points":

- choose one successful teaching strategy to enhance

- implement embodied AI support gradually

- document effects on teaching and learning

- adjust based on observations

Week 4: Expansion and Refinement

- add new enhancement points

- deepen successful integrations

- share effective approaches

- support colleague growth

Throughout our journey, remember these key insights from successful teams:

- **Building support networks:**

    o form small collaboration groups

    o schedule regular check-ins

    o share challenges and successes

    o celebrate small victories

- **Maintaining balance:**
  - preserve effective teaching practices
  - enhance natural learning patterns
  - support physical engagement
  - trust your teaching instincts

- **Creating sustainable growth:**
  - start small but think systematically
  - document successful approaches
  - build on what works
  - share your learning

- **Success emerges through**
  - thoughtful observation
  - gradual implementation
  - collaborative support
  - continuous reflection

The goal is to create what one successful team called "living teaching practices"—approaches that naturally blend traditional wisdom with embodied AI support.

Through careful attention to natural learning patterns, thoughtful technology integration, and strong support networks, embodied AI becomes an organic extension of effective teaching practice. Keep your focus on

- supporting natural learning

- enhancing student engagement

- building teacher confidence

- celebrating growth moments

Success in this journey comes from fostering spaces of possibility while creating enactive learning environments where technology enhances human potential. Trust your teaching wisdom, lean on your support network, and let your integration of embodied AI unfold naturally through thoughtful practice and collaborative exploration.

The transformation happens in small gestures, meaningful steps forward down a path of discovery where unknown learning experiences unfold unexpected pathways.

Chapter 4:

Implementing Embodied AI in the Classroom

Before diving into implementation, let's reflect on your path so far. Consider how your initial exploration of embodied AI has brought you here, whether the information in *Embodied AI Education: Unlocking Human Potential Through Enactive Learning* has shaped your vision for implementation, or you've come across this guide on your own:

- What aspects of embodied learning first caught your attention?

- Which challenges in your current practice led you to explore AI support?

- How do your students already demonstrate physical understanding?

- What three elements of your curriculum seem most ready for embodied AI integration?

For example, one science teacher noticed students naturally using gestures to explain molecular movement. This observation led her to explore how embodied AI could enhance these natural physical demonstrations of understanding.

Integrating Embodied AI Into Lesson Planning

The journey from traditional to AI-enhanced planning begins with recognizing how technology can amplify your natural teaching rhythms. Rather than forcing AI into existing plans, look for opportunities where it can support your teaching strengths while opening spaces of possibility for unexpected enactive learning experiences.

Current Tools and Practices

Many teachers already use tools that can serve as stepping stones to embodied AI integration:

- digital planning platforms like Planboard or Chalk

- collaborative tools like Google Workspace

- assessment systems like Kahoot! or Nearpod

- learning management systems like Canvas or Schoology

The key is building from these familiar foundations toward more embodied approaches.

Exercise: Lesson Planning Enhancement Pathway

Objective: Create a systematic approach to incorporating embodied AI while maintaining an authentic teaching presence.

Initial reflection: Consider your current practice:

- Where do your students show understanding through movement?

- Which lessons naturally incorporate physical engagement?

- What planning tools do you already use effectively?

- How might embodied AI enhance these existing practices?

For example, one mathematics teacher noticed students unconsciously using hand gestures while explaining geometric concepts. This observation led her to explore how embodied AI could track and support these natural physical expressions of understanding.

Implementation Timeline

Week 1: Current Practice Analysis

Begin by examining your existing tools and approaches.

Morning documentation:

- What planning tools currently work well for you?

- How do you already incorporate movement in lessons?

- Where do students naturally demonstrate physical understanding?

- Which parts of planning feel most time-consuming?

For example, many teachers find success starting with familiar tools like Pear Deck or Nearpod, gradually adding embodied AI features to enhance the physical interaction patterns they already track.

Afternoon integration planning:

- Which current digital tools could evolve to include embodied AI?

- How might AI support your physical teaching approaches?

- What natural movement patterns could AI help track?

- Where could technology enhance rather than replace physical interaction?

Week 2: Tool Integration

Choose one familiar tool to enhance with embodied AI capabilities. For instance, if you already use classroom response systems, consider how adding movement tracking could deepen understanding of student engagement.

Sample integration path:

- **Day 1–2:** Connect embodied AI features to existing tools.

- **Day 3–4:** Practice with familiar lesson content.

- **Day 5:** Create your first movement-enhanced lesson.

- **Days 6–10:** Refine based on student response.

Building From Current Practice

Most teachers already personalize instruction through observation and intuition. Consider how you currently

- Notice student engagement through body language.

- Adapt to physical signs of understanding or confusion.

- Respond to natural movement patterns.

- Support different learning styles.

For example, one elementary teacher already used flexible seating and movement breaks. She built on this by incorporating embodied AI to track which movement patterns best supported different learners.

Exercise: Personalized Learning Implementation

Objective: Enhance your existing differentiation strategies with embodied AI while preserving authentic relationships.

Phase 1: Understanding Your Foundation

Start by mapping your current personalization approaches:

Week 1: Student Learning Patterns

Begin with familiar observation tools like

- anecdotal notes in digital planners

- video recordings of student interactions

- simple movement pattern tracking

- existing student response systems

Real classroom example: A middle school team started by using their existing Seesaw portfolios to document physical demonstrations of learning, later adding embodied AI analysis to identify successful patterns.

Essential questions:

- How do different students show understanding through movement?

- What physical cues indicate engagement versus confusion?

- Which existing tools help you track student responses?

- How might embodied AI enhance your current observation methods?

Week 2: Building on Success

Consider how to enhance effective practices:

- Which current differentiation strategies work best?

- How could embodied AI support these approaches?

- What patterns might AI help you recognize?

- Where could technology provide deeper insights?

Tool integration example: One teacher began by adding motion tracking to her existing classroom response system, helping her identify physical patterns of engagement she hadn't noticed before.

Weeks 3–4: Thoughtful Implementation

First 5 days—Starting with strength: Begin with one successful teaching approach you'd like to enhance. For example, if students respond well to movement-based math activities, start there:

- How does your current approach engage students physically?

- What patterns could embodied AI help track?

- Which existing tools could you build upon?

- What additional insights would be most valuable?

Real classroom example: A third-grade teacher began by adding embodied AI features to her existing Number Talks routine, tracking how students naturally used gestures to explain mathematical thinking.

Days 6-15—Expanding thoughtfully: Build on early successes by asking

- Which elements of your enhanced approach work best?

- What unexpected insights has the technology provided?

- How are students responding to different features?

- Where might you expand next?

Current tools to consider: Many teachers find success building on

- ClassDojo for behavior patterns

- Explain Everything for movement capture

- Screencastify for gesture analysis

- Flipgrid for physical demonstration tracking

Project-Based Learning With Embodied AI

Building on Existing Projects

Start by examining successful projects you already run:

- Where do students naturally incorporate movement?

- How do they physically demonstrate understanding?

- What collaboration patterns emerge?

- Which tools currently support project work?

Example from practice: One science teacher enhanced her existing ecosystem project by adding embodied AI to track how students physically modeled environmental relationships, building on her existing use of project documentation tools.

Exercise: Project Evolution Workshop

Objective: Enhance existing project-based learning with embodied AI while maintaining student creativity and ownership.

Phase 1: Current Project Analysis

Begin with a successful project you already run.

Week 1: Mapping Current Practice

Document existing patterns using familiar tools:

- How do students currently document progress?

- Which digital tools support collaboration?

- What physical interactions occur naturally?

- Where do students demonstrate understanding through movement?

Real example: A history teacher who used Timeline JS for project documentation added embodied AI features to capture how students physically reenacted historical events, enhancing their existing digital storytelling approach.

Common tools to build upon:

- Padlet for visual project mapping

- Trello for progress tracking

- WeVideo for movement capture

- Google Sites for project portfolios

Week 2: Thoughtful Integration

Questions to guide tool selection:

- How might embodied AI enhance existing project documentation?

- Which current tools could expand to include movement tracking?

- What physical patterns would be valuable to capture?

- How can technology support natural collaboration?

Success story: One middle school team enhanced their existing MakerSpace projects by adding embodied AI to track student movement patterns during design and construction, building on their familiar use of project management tools.

Assessment With Embodied AI

Starting With Current Assessment Practices

Consider your existing assessment tools:

- How do you currently document physical demonstrations of learning?

- Which digital tools help track student progress?

- What movement-based assessments already work well?

- Where could embodied AI provide deeper insights?

Exercise: Assessment Evolution Workshop

Phase 1: Building From Strength

Start with successful assessment approaches.

Week 1: Current Practice Enhancement

Many teachers begin with familiar tools like

- Seesaw portfolios for capturing physical demonstrations

- Rubric creators like ForAllRubrics

- Google Forms for quick assessments

- Screen recording tools for movement analysis

Real example: A PE teacher enhanced her existing skills assessment by adding embodied AI to her regular video analysis routine, providing deeper insights into movement patterns and skill development.

Phase 2: Integration Planning

Questions to guide enhancement:

- How could embodied AI deepen your current assessment insights?

- Which existing tools could incorporate movement tracking?

- What physical demonstrations of learning matter most?

- How might technology support more natural assessment?

Classroom Management With Embodied AI

Enhancing Current Management Systems

Begin by examining effective practices:

- Which digital tools already support your management?

- How do you currently track student engagement?

- What movement patterns indicate classroom flow?

- Where might embodied AI provide helpful insights?

Common tools to build upon:

- ClassDojo for behavior tracking

- Google Classroom for organization

- LanSchool for activity monitoring

- smart lighting systems for environment control

Success story: One fourth-grade team enhanced their existing classroom management system by adding embodied AI to track natural transition patterns, building on their familiar use of digital behavior monitoring.

End-Of-Chapter Implementation Reflection

Tool Assessment

Consider your implementation journey:

1. **Current tools**

   o Which existing tools provided the best foundation for embodied AI integration?

   o How did familiar technologies help ease the transition?

   o What unexpected capabilities did you discover in current tools?

2. **Impact analysis**

   o Where did embodied AI most enhance your teaching?

   o Which tools created more work than value?

   o What surprised you about the integration process?

   o How has your practice evolved?

3. **Student response**

   o How did learners react to enhanced tools?

   o Which features supported natural learning patterns?

   o What unexpected benefits emerged?

   o Where might you adjust your approach?

4. **Next steps**

   o Which additional tools might you investigate?

   o How could you deepen successful integrations?

   o What patterns deserve more attention?

   o Where might you explore next?

Finding Your Flow: Tools and Resources

Rather than providing a fixed list of tools that may quickly become outdated, we encourage educators to explore and discover tools that best support their unique pedagogical flow. For example, one high school English teacher shares their current toolkit for enhancing learning flow:

- using Claude AI for complex differentiation and text transformation

- creating quick resources with Diffit

- knowledge checking through Quizizz

- lesson planning with Google Notebook LM

- providing personalized feedback via Brisk AI

Remember: The specific tools matter less than how they support your natural teaching rhythm and enhance student learning experiences.

For updated tool reviews and recommendations, visit EdSurge at www.edsurge.com which features up-to-date current coverage of the rapidly evolving edtech space.

The key is finding tools that

- Enhance your natural teaching flow.

- Support embodied learning experiences.

- Adapt to your unique context.

- Grow with your practice.

Rather than following prescriptive tool lists, engage with professional learning networks where educators actively share their experiences with emerging tools and approaches. Success comes through discovering what works in your specific context while maintaining focus on pedagogical flow and student engagement.

Chapter 5:

Embodied AI for School

Administration

In the bustling hallways of modern schools, a quiet revolution unfolds. The integration of embodied AI into classroom practice demands more than just technological adoption—it requires thoughtful administrative support that enhances, rather than disrupts, teachers' natural instructional flow. Through careful observation and strategic implementation, administrators can help educators identify those precious moments where AI meaningfully supports learning while preserving the vibrant physical and social dynamics that make classrooms come alive.

Successful integration begins with deep reflection. Before diving into implementation, administrators should consider several critical questions:

- How might we create spaces where teachers can organically explore embodied AI?

- What underlying support structures will help maintain the delicate rhythm of teaching?

- In what ways can professional development honor and build upon existing teaching wisdom?

- Where can we eliminate barriers that impede natural integration?

The Art of Supporting Natural Integration

True integration emerges through understanding and nurturing technology that augments natural teaching rhythms. Akram et al. (2022) illuminate how thoughtful administrators have successfully supported teachers across various disciplines in identifying and fostering natural learning patterns through strategic AI integration.

Consider the multifaceted role administrators must play:

- carving out protected exploration time in busy schedules

- empowering teacher-led observation initiatives

- securing and allocating necessary resources

- dismantling administrative barriers

- celebrating organic discoveries as they emerge

A compelling example unfolded in one high school's chemistry department. When teachers noticed students spontaneously using specific gestures to demonstrate molecular bonding, administrators responded with remarkable agility:

- quickly provided motion-tracking technology to capture these natural learning moments

- created dedicated spaces for sharing best practices

- facilitated cross-department collaboration opportunities

- fiercely protected teacher innovation time

Understanding Natural Teaching Patterns:

Through an Administrator's Lens

Before rushing to implement AI tools, skilled administrators help teachers document and understand their current practices. This process requires asking thoughtful questions that probe different aspects of the teaching experience.

For Classroom Observation

- How do your teachers naturally adjust their teaching rhythm throughout the day?

- Where do those magical moments of deep student engagement typically occur?

- What kinds of support do teachers need to maintain their instructional flow?

- How might administrative tasks be streamlined to protect valuable teaching time?

For Supporting Physical Learning

- In what creative ways do your teachers utilize classroom space?

- Where does natural movement emerge during learning activities?

- Which resources would best support embodied learning approaches?

- How can facility decisions enhance rather than hinder teaching flow?

Exercise: Administrative Support Enhancement

Objective: Develop systematic approaches to supporting teachers while maintaining their authentic teaching presence.

Let's establish a clear timeline for implementation.

Week 1: Current Support Analysis

Probe deeply into existing practices:

- Which administrative tasks most frequently interrupt the teaching flow?

- How can required documentation be streamlined?

- Where do teachers need greater flexibility?

- What resources would naturally enhance teaching patterns?

Document your current support process through multiple lenses.

- **Time protection:**

    o How effectively are you sheltering teaching time?

    o Where can administrative duties be reduced or eliminated?

    o When do teachers have genuine space for innovation?

    o What meeting structures best support natural collaboration?

- **Resource allocation:**

    o How are you supporting creative teaching approaches?

    o Where might additional resources enhance natural flow?

- What technology truly serves teaching rhythm?

- How can budget decisions protect instructional time?

Supporting Personalized Instruction Through Embodied AI

Beyond basic implementation lies a more nuanced challenge: helping teachers maintain genuine human connections while leveraging AI support. Agyeman and Aphane's (2024) research reveals how thoughtful administrative leadership enables teachers to identify learning patterns and adapt instruction while deepening student relationships.

The delicate balance between technology and human interaction raises several crucial questions:

Questions for Supporting Teacher–Student Relationships

Through the quiet moments of classroom observation and teacher feedback, administrators should reflect

- How might scheduling decisions foster deeper student connections?

- Where can administrative flexibility enhance personalization opportunities?

- What resources truly help teachers maintain their natural instructional rhythm?

- In what ways can observation protocols honor organic teaching patterns?

Exercise: Supporting Personalized Learning Implementation

Objective: Craft administrative structures that empower teachers to harness embodied AI while preserving authentic relationships.

Week 1: Understanding Your Teachers' Needs

Dive deep into existing practices:

- Observe how different teachers naturally personalize their instruction

- Identify points where administrative requirements disrupt the teaching flow

- Explore support structures that could enhance natural differentiation

- Examine how observation processes might better celebrate teacher wisdom

Week 2: Developing Support Systems

From the foundation of understanding action emerges:

Administrative framework: Transform traditional structures to support natural flow:

- Redesign master schedules to protect teaching rhythm.

- Reimagine meeting structures to enhance organic collaboration.

- Create professional development that truly serves teacher needs, through input from those it is meant to support.

- Develop evaluation systems that honor natural teaching patterns.

Resource allocation: Make strategic decisions that preserve teaching authenticity:

- Select tools that genuinely support teaching rhythm.

- Align budget decisions with instructional flow protection.

- Consider facility changes that enhance learning spaces.

- Invest in technology that serves real pedagogical needs.

Nurturing Project-Based Learning With Embodied AI

The intersection of project-based learning and embodied AI offers unique opportunities for innovation. Martinez's (2022) case study sheds light on how thoughtful administrative support can enhance project-based learning while preserving teacher autonomy and student creativity.

Successful administrators continually explore

- How scheduling might better support extended learning experiences

- Where facility decisions could enhance project work

- Which resources enable truly natural inquiry

- Ways evaluation systems can honor authentic project-based learning

Exercise: Project-Based Learning Support Framework

Objective: Create administrative structures that nurture organic project development while leveraging embodied AI capabilities.

Phase 1: Environment Assessment

Examine your current project support systems:

- Map existing project spaces and resources.

- Identify natural collaboration points.

- Document successful project patterns.

Note barriers to extended learning.

Phase 2: Enhanced Support Development

Build upon successful patterns:

- Design flexible scheduling options.

- Create adaptive resource allocation systems.

- Develop project-friendly assessment approaches.

- Establish innovation support networks.

Building Sustainable Support Systems

The journey of administrative support for embodied AI requires continuous evolution. Consider implementing the following long-term strategies.

Regular Reflection Cycles

Establish quarterly review periods to

- Assess support effectiveness.

- Identify emerging needs.

- Celebrate successful innovations.

- Adjust resource allocation.

Community Engagement

Build broader support through

- parent education initiatives

- community partnership development

- student voice incorporation

- teacher leadership opportunities

Future Planning

Look ahead by

- anticipating emerging needs

- planning resource development

- building capacity for growth

- creating sustainable support structures

Looking Forward-Opening Spaces of Possibility

Remember that administrative support serves as the foundation for successful embodied AI integration. Through thoughtful leadership and strategic support, administrators can create environments where technology enhances the human elements of education.

The most successful implementations emerge from administrators who

- Listen deeply to teacher needs.

- Respond flexibly to emerging patterns.

- Protect natural teaching rhythms.

- Celebrate organic innovation.

- Build sustainable support systems.

As we transition to exploring professional development in the next chapter, carry forward this understanding: True administrative leadership in the age of embodied AI isn't about controlling change—it's about cultivating environments where change can flourish naturally. The future of education emerges not from top-down mandates but from the ground up, nurtured by administrators who understand that their most powerful role is creating spaces where teachers and students can discover new possibilities together. In this delicate balance between support and freedom, between structure and flexibility, we find the path toward educational experiences that honor both technological innovation and the deeply human art of teaching.

Chapter 6:

Professional Development for

Embodied AI Integration

A science teacher leans over her colleague's desk during morning prep time, excitedly sharing how her students naturally demonstrated molecular bonding through movement. Down the hall, a math teacher records a successful moment where embodied AI helped track geometric understanding through student gestures. These organic learning moments, emerging naturally from daily teaching practice, represent the future of professional development for embodied AI integration.

The transformation of professional learning begins with a fundamental shift in our understanding: The most powerful development happens in these natural moments of teacher exchange. Hwang and Chen (2024) reveal how schools successfully shifted from traditional workshop models to learning flow spaces—environments where professional growth emerges organically from teachers' daily practice.

This organic approach to professional development allows for implementation across diverse educational settings. Consider how one district transformed its approach: Instead of scheduling monthly technology workshops, it created morning exploration spaces; teachers would gather informally before school, sharing coffee and discoveries about its embodied AI journey. A math teacher might demonstrate how students naturally used gestures to explain algebraic concepts, while a physical education instructor would share observations about movement patterns during skill learning activities.

To implement such natural learning environments in your own setting, consider the following structured yet flexible approach.

Exercise: Creating Learning Flow Spaces

Objective: Design professional development that supports natural teacher growth while maintaining instructional flow.

Setup requirements:

- dedicated collaboration space

- recording equipment for success sharing

- digital platform for resource collection

- protected time for teacher exploration

Implementation Steps

Week 1: Pattern Observation

- Document when teachers naturally collaborate.

- Note preferred sharing times and spaces.

- Identify existing successful practices.

- Map organic learning networks.

Week 2: Flow Space Development

- Create flexible meeting areas.

- Establish sharing protocols.

- Design documentation systems.

- Set up support structures.

Deepening Professional Learning Through Cross-Disciplinary Exchange

The power of organic professional development reveals itself most clearly in unexpected collaborations. One high school's science and physical education departments discovered shared insights about movement-based learning. The PE teacher's expertise in analyzing physical patterns helped the physics teacher develop more intuitive ways for students to embody concepts like momentum and force. Meanwhile, the physics teacher's understanding of motion principles enhanced the PE teacher's ability to help students visualize and improve their athletic movements.

This natural collaboration led to movement-science synthesis sessions, where teachers from different disciplines regularly shared observations about how students physically demonstrated understanding. These cross-disciplinary insights often sparked innovative teaching approaches that neither department would have discovered in isolation.

Exercise: Cross-Disciplinary Learning Flow

Objective: Create opportunities for meaningful exchange between different subject areas while maintaining natural teaching rhythms.

Setup requirements:

- flexible meeting spaces that accommodate movement

- simple recording tools for capturing physical demonstrations

- shared digital platform for cross-discipline resources

- protected time for collaborative exploration

Implementation Process

Phase 1: Discovery (Weeks 1–2)

- Identify natural connection points between disciplines.

- Document shared movement patterns across subjects.

- Map overlapping teaching challenges.

- Note unexpected learning parallels.

Phase 2: Integration (Weeks 3–4)

- Create collaborative teaching experiments.

- Document cross-disciplinary insights.

- Develop a shared vocabulary for movement patterns.

- Build a resource collection of successful approaches.

The success of these learning flow spaces depends heavily on understanding and supporting the natural rhythms of professional growth. In fact, the rhythm of professional development rarely follows a preset schedule. Powerful learning emerges during those unexpected times when a colleague pops into a classroom to share a breakthrough or when a spontaneous hallway conversation would lead to a new teaching insight.

Recognizing the value of these spontaneous learning opportunities, successful administrators have developed strategies to protect and nurture them. They create flexible coverage systems allowing teachers to observe each other's classes and establish digital sharing platforms where educators can quickly capture and share successful moments.

To capitalize on these natural learning patterns, consider implementing the following framework.

Exercise: Building Learning Rhythms

Objective: Create sustainable systems for continuous professional growth that honor natural teaching flows.

Setup requirements:

- flexible coverage schedule

- quick-capture documentation tools

- digital sharing platform

- protected collaboration time

Implementation Process

Phase 1: Establishing Flow Patterns

- Map natural collaboration times.

- Identify sharing opportunities.

- Create coverage systems.

- Design support structures.

Phase 2: Nurturing Growth Spaces

Weeks 1–2: Initial Implementation

- Launch quick-share protocols.

- Test coverage systems.

- Document success patterns.

- Gather teacher feedback.

- Adjust based on usage patterns.

- Expand successful approaches.

- Address emerging needs.

- Celebrate enactive learning moments.

Enhancing Digital Documentation of Physical Learning

As learning communities develop, the challenge of capturing physical teaching moments becomes increasingly important. One way to do this is the development of a movement memory system—a combination of quick-capture tools and reflection protocols that helps teachers document and share physical teaching breakthroughs without disrupting their natural flow.

The approach includes

- strategic placement of easily accessible recording devices

- simple gesture-based activation of recording tools

- quick-tag system for categorizing movement patterns

- automated sharing with relevant colleague groups

This system will evolve through careful attention to when and how teachers naturally wanted to capture moments of discovery. Rather than imposing rigid documentation requirements, create protocols that feel like natural extensions of teaching practice, especially when implementing hands-on lab or group activities to enact processes, for example, learning about protein synthesis.

Exercise: Movement Memory Development

Objective: Create intuitive systems for documenting physical teaching insights while maintaining instructional flow.

Setup elements:

- easy-access recording stations

- quick-capture mobile tools

- automatic categorization system

- seamless sharing protocols

Implementation Timeline

Month 1: System Design

- Map natural documentation moments.

- Test various capture tools.

- Develop simple categorization approaches.

- Create initial sharing protocols.

Month 2: Integration

- Deploy pilot capture stations.

- Train early adopters.

- Gather usage patterns.

- Refine based on feedback.

As these rhythms become established, natural learning communities often emerge around shared experiences and challenges. A powerful example of this organic development can be seen in how a group of math teachers began meeting informally during lunch to share their discoveries about how students physically demonstrated geometric concepts. This organic gathering evolved into what they called their "movement mathematics circle"—a vibrant community of practice that eventually expanded to include science teachers interested in physical demonstrations of scientific principles.

Exercise: Nurturing Learning Communities

Objective: Support the natural development of teacher learning networks while maintaining focus on embodied learning experiences.

Setup elements:

- common planning spaces

- cross-disciplinary gathering areas

- digital connection platforms

- resource sharing systems

Initial Development

Week 1: Community Mapping

- Identify existing collaboration patterns.

- Note natural teacher leaders.

- Document successful sharing practices.

- Recognize cross-disciplinary connections.

The power of these communities becomes evident in practice. For instance, a high school science department discovered their most effective community building happened in what they called "flow zones"—areas where teachers could casually demonstrate successful embodied learning approaches during prep periods. The physics teacher might show how students used movement to understand force concepts, sparking ideas for the biology teacher about demonstrating cellular processes through motion.

Integrating Formal Educational Pathways

While organic professional development forms the foundation of embodied AI integration, formal educational programs offer valuable structured pathways for deeper exploration. The synergy between daily practice and formal study creates rich opportunities for advancement.

University Programs Supporting Embodied AI Integration

Several universities have developed programs specifically addressing AI integration in education:

- Stanford University's Learning, Design, and Technology program emphasizes embodied learning approaches.

- Columbia Teachers College offers specializations in AI and education.

- MIT's Media Lab explores innovative intersections of movement, learning, and technology.

- University of Washington's Learning Sciences program focuses on embodied cognition research.

Research Through Practice

Many teachers discover their most compelling research questions through daily classroom experiences. Consider these examples:

- a PE teacher's observations of movement patterns led to a master's thesis on embodied mathematics learning

- an elementary teacher's documentation of student gestures became the foundation for doctoral research on embodied literacy development

- a music teacher's experiments with AI-enhanced movement tracking evolved into a university research partnership

By combining formal study with practical experience, educators create powerful feedback loops between theory and practice. Their research not only advances their own understanding but contributes to the broader field of embodied learning.

Fostering Global Learning Connections

The power of natural professional development extends beyond individual schools through flow networks—organic connections between educators exploring embodied AI across different contexts. One suburban American school discovered unexpected insights through its partnership with a rural Indian school, where teachers had developed innovative approaches to movement-based learning with minimal technology.

These cross-cultural connections revealed universal patterns in how students physically demonstrate understanding while also highlighting unique cultural variations in movement expression. The resulting exchange enriched both communities' approaches to embodied learning.

Exercise: Global Flow Network Development

Objective: Create sustainable international learning connections that enhance local teaching practice.

Setup requirements:

- reliable communication platforms

- shared documentation tools

- translation resources

- flexible meeting times

Implementation Process

Phase 1: Connection Building

- Identify potential partner schools.

- Establish communication protocols.

- Create shared documentation spaces.

- Develop a cultural exchange framework.

Phase 2: Knowledge Exchange

- Share successful teaching patterns.

- Document cultural variations.

- Build collaborative resources.

- Celebrate shared discoveries.

As these communities develop, measuring their impact requires a new approach to assessment. Traditional professional development metrics often miss the subtle yet powerful indicators of teacher growth. Look for flow evidence—natural demonstrations of how professional learning enhances teaching practice.

When observing impact, consider these key questions:

- Where do you see teachers spontaneously sharing new approaches?

- How has classroom movement and interaction evolved?

- What unexpected collaborations have emerged?

- Where do students demonstrate deeper engagement?

Exercise: Authentic Impact Documentation

Objective: Create natural ways to capture and celebrate professional growth while maintaining teaching flow.

Documentation tools:

- quick-capture video system

- digital success journal

- sharing platform

- reflection space

Implementation Timeline

Month 1: Establishing Baseline Flow

- Document current teaching patterns.

- Note collaboration frequency.

- Map student engagement.

- Record learning interactions.

Evaluating Long-Term Pedagogical Impact

The success of organic professional development reveals itself not just in immediate teaching improvements but transformation—fundamental shifts in how teachers approach their practice. One district tracked these changes through teaching evolution mapping documenting how individual teachers' approaches evolved over multiple years of embodied AI integration.

Their observations revealed several key patterns:

- Initial changes often appeared small but led to significant transformations.

- Cross-disciplinary influences accelerated innovation.

- Teacher confidence grew through organic exploration.

- Student engagement increased as teachers found their flow.

As with any significant change, some teachers may initially hesitate to embrace embodied AI integration. However, successful schools have learned to view this hesitation not as an obstacle, but as a natural part of the learning flow, acknowledging that experienced teachers' hesitation often stems from a deep understanding of learning rhythms.

This perspective shift has led to valuable insights. Consider how one veteran English teacher's initial hesitation led to important discoveries about maintaining student discussion flow when integrating embodied AI. Her concerns about technology interrupting natural classroom dialogue helped develop more organic implementation approaches that opened exciting learning opportunities for her existing teaching patterns.

Exercise: Supporting Natural Integration

Objective: Create supportive pathways for teachers to explore embodied AI while honoring their established teaching wisdom.

Setup considerations:

- low-pressure exploration spaces

- peer support networks

- flexible trial periods

- protected practice time

Implementation Flow: Understanding Teaching Wisdom

Weeks 1–2: Deep Listening

- Host informal sharing sessions.

- Document teacher insights.

- Note successful practices.

- Identify core values.

Weeks 3–4: Bridge Building

- Connect existing practices with new possibilities.

- Identify natural integration points.

- Create safe exploration spaces.

- Celebrate small successes.

This approach has proven successful across various settings. A middle school math department found particular success with what they called their wisdom integration approach. Rather than pushing for immediate adoption, they encouraged teachers to first document their most effective teaching moments. Then, they explored how embodied AI might naturally strengthen these already successful practices.

Throughout this integration process, keep these essential questions in mind:

- How can we protect what already works well?

- Where might technology naturally enhance current practices?

- What aspects of successful teaching need preservation?

- How can we support organic exploration?

The journey toward embodied AI integration succeeds when we recognize that meaningful change emerges through natural teaching rhythms, opening new ways of knowing and being. By creating supportive conditions for exploration while honoring established teaching wisdom, we enable professional growth that promotes the natural flow of learning. Success that emerges through thoughtful integration truly honors teaching, wisdom, and learning potential.

Chapter 7:

Data Management and Privacy

Every day in schools across the country, educators navigate an invisible landscape of data—not just grades and attendance records, but now streams of information from AI systems tracking student movements, learning patterns, and interactions. This new dimension of educational data brings both opportunities and responsibilities. Opportunities emerge through the complex interplay of physical, social, and technological elements in educational spaces (Almasri, 2024).

Understanding these data patterns requires sustained observation over multiple cycles. While Chapter 6 focused on the observational practices that inform teaching, here we examine how to systematically collect, protect, and leverage this data within a formal infrastructure. Effective data management emerges through continuous observational learning, as patterns of pedagogical practice vary significantly across different environments, subjects, and teaching strategies (Giannakos et al., 2019).

The transformation of school data practices often begins with fundamental questions that emerge from daily practice: How does this movement data enhance learning? How do we ensure data privacy while maintaining educational value? How do we capture the subtle patterns that experienced teachers naturally observe? These questions spark essential dialogues about balancing innovation with protection.

Before diving into specific practices, let's establish a clear implementation timeline that will guide our discussion:

- **Year 1: Foundation building:**

    - traditional academic data infrastructure

    - basic movement-tracking pilots

- ○ essential security frameworks

  - ○ core privacy protocols

- **Years 2–3: Expansion phase:**

  - ○ advanced movement patterns

  - ○ interaction data integration

  - ○ enhanced security measures

  - ○ comprehensive compliance systems

- **Years 3–4: Full integration:**

  - ○ complex behavioral analytics

  - ○ cross-system correlations

  - ○ advanced governance structures

  - ○ predictive modeling capabilities

With this roadmap in mind, let's explore each aspect of data management in detail.

Understanding Data Requirements for Embodied AI Systems

Traditional data collection focused on grades, attendance, and basic demographics. Embodied AI introduces new dimensions—movement patterns, interaction data, and physical engagement metrics—requiring an enactive approach to data collection and management (Zhang & Aslan, 2021).

As we transition from traditional to embodied AI data collection, developing a comprehensive data ecosystem becomes crucial for long-term success.

Flow pedagogy demonstrates how successful data management emerges through careful attention to natural information patterns (Goh & Yang, 2021). When applying systems theory to educational data management, mapping how teachers naturally document student progress reveals patterns that shape entire approaches to data collection (Bond et al., 2020).

This systematic approach builds upon, but differs from, the observational practices discussed in Chapter 6. Let's explore how to implement these systems through a structured exercise that aligns with our multiyear timeline.

Exercise: Data Requirement Mapping

Objective: Create a comprehensive understanding of your AI system's data needs while respecting privacy and educational value.

Initial Discovery Year (Year 1)

Phase 1: Current Practice Observation (2 Months)

Begin by observing how teachers naturally track student progress. The most valuable insights often emerge not from formal assessments but from teachers' observations of student movement and engagement during learning activities.

Successful implementations demonstrate the value of maintaining what complexity theory terms a data journal, recording:

- Natural assessment moments

- Informal progress tracking

- Student interaction patterns

- Movement and engagement observations

Phase 2: Pattern Recognition (2 Months)

Unlike the general observations discussed in Chapter 6, here we focus on systematic data collection:

- Begin with traditional academic data.

- Pilot basic movement tracking in select classrooms.

- Focus on 2–3 key behavioral metrics.

Phase 3: Initial System Design (2 Months)

Living data guidelines provide frameworks that support natural teaching while gathering necessary information (Nguyen et al., 2020).

Extended Implementation (Years 2–3)

Building on the foundation established in Year 1:

- Track student engagement through movement patterns.

- Assess understanding through physical responses.

- Adjust instruction based on behavioral cues.

The challenge becomes capturing this intuitive knowledge without disrupting its natural flow. These patterns emerge naturally rather than through rigid collection protocols (Schilhab & Groth, 2024).

Data Protection Framework

As schools develop their data collection processes, the critical question of protection naturally emerges. While gathering valuable information about student learning patterns, we must ensure this data remains secure and private. Let's explore how to build robust security measures that protect while preserving educational value.

Educational data privacy security is more than protecting information—it's about preserving the joy of learning while ensuring student safety (National Forum on Education Statistics, 2016). This understanding shapes our approach to security implementation throughout our multiyear timeline.

Exercise: Security Framework Development

Objective: Create robust data protection systems that maintain the natural flow of teaching and learning.

Initial Implementation Year (Year 1)

Phase 1: Protection Assessment (3 Months)

The key to securing educational data is understanding how information moves through school environments. The most sensitive data vulnerabilities often occur not in main systems but in seemingly innocent classroom applications used for daily instruction.

Data journey maps provide essential structure (Cohen et al., 2022):

- Track information flow between systems.

- Identify natural security checkpoints.

- Note where data naturally accumulates.

- Document current protection practices.

Phase 2: Basic Security Implementation (3 Months)

Focus on establishing foundational protection measures:

- basic data protection protocols

- essential security measures

- core privacy frameworks

Phase 3: System Integration (6 Months)

Effective security frameworks emerge through sustained observation of how data naturally flows through educational environments.

Extended Development (Years 2–3)

Building on the foundation established in Year 1:

- enhanced protection systems

- advanced security features

- comprehensive privacy measures

Compliance Framework

With security measures taking shape, we must consider how these protections align with legal requirements while maintaining educational effectiveness.

The key to securing educational data is understanding how information moves through school environments. The most sensitive data vulnerabilities often occur not in main systems but in seemingly innocent classroom applications used for daily instruction.

Data journey maps provide essential structure (Cohen et al., 2022):

- Track information flow between systems.

- Identify natural security checkpoints.

- Note where data naturally accumulates.

- Document current protection practices.

Effective compliance in educational data management emerges from understanding how regulatory requirements naturally align with good educational practice. This transforms compliance into a framework for better educational practice.

Exercise: Compliance Integration

Objective: Develop compliance systems that integrate with educational practice.

Quality compliance systems emerge through multiple cycles of observation and adjustment, as patterns of data use vary across different educational contexts.

The Integration Journey: A Three-Year Implementation Plan

Year 1: Foundation Building

- **Understanding requirements:**

    o establishing core compliance protocols

    o setting up essential documentation systems

    o aligning with basic regulations

- **Practice integration:**

  - integrating data review into teaching practices

  - building collaborative planning routines

  - developing professional development frameworks

- **Community engagement:**

  - initiating stakeholder meetings

  - establishing family communication channels

  - creating feedback systems

Years 2–3: Advanced Implementation

- expanding to advanced compliance measures

- developing comprehensive documentation

- achieving full regulatory integration

- deepening community partnerships

- refining ethical frameworks

- enhancing data protection practices

As compliance systems mature, we must consider the ethical implications of our data practices and how they align with our educational mission.

Ethical Framework

Effective data use is a balance between student welfare and analytical power. This insight aligns with cognitive research in embodied learning systems (Schilhab & Groth, 2024).

Exercise: Ethical Framework Development

Objective: Create guidelines for data use that prioritize student benefit while ensuring protection.

Initial Implementation Year (Year 1)

Phase 1: Understanding Impact (4 Months)

Giannakos et al. (2019) stress that constant diligence is needed in analyzing data and its effects on student learning. The most effective interventions come from combining AI insights with human observation—neither alone tells the complete story.

Impact journals are essential tools:

- Record when data insights led to improved support.

- Note instances where human observation proved crucial.

- Document unexpected benefits and concerns.

- Track student and family responses to data use.

Phase 2: Guidelines Development (4 Months)

Focus on establishing foundational principles:

- basic ethical guidelines

- core protection principles

- essential impact measures

Phase 3: Framework Integration (4 Months)

Living ethical principles evolve with community needs while maintaining clear boundaries (Schilhab & Groth, 2024).

Extended Development (Years 2–3)

Building on the foundation established in Year 1:

- advanced ethical frameworks

- comprehensive protection

- deep impact analysis

Governance Framework

A strong governance system ensures that ethical principles, security measures, and data practices work together effectively. This framework should

- Define clear roles and responsibilities for data oversight.

- Establish regular review cycles for all policies.

- Create transparent processes for updating guidelines.

- Build feedback channels between administrators, teachers, and families.

Such a system helps schools

- Maintain consistent ethical standards across all departments.

- Respond quickly to new challenges or concerns.

- Keep policies aligned with evolving community needs.

- Balance innovation with student protection.

As Schilhab & Groth (2024) note, effective governance allows ethical principles to evolve naturally with community needs while maintaining essential protective boundaries. This dynamic approach ensures that schools can adapt to new opportunities while staying true to their core commitment to student well-being.

Effective educational data governance emerges from viewing data management as a community responsibility rather than just a technical challenge. Success comes from understanding your school's unique needs and values within the broader context of data protection requirements.

Exercise: Governance Evolution

Objective: Create a governance framework that supports educational goals while ensuring proper data stewardship.

Initial Implementation Year (Year 1)

Phase 1: Community Engagement (4 Months)

Community engagement starts with structured conversations about hopes and concerns regarding student data (Cohen et al., 2022). As demonstrated in community engagement, parents often focus less on data collection itself and more on how it will support their children's learning.

Key discussion areas for "responsive governance":

- how data supports student success

- boundaries for data use

- access and control preferences

- protection priorities

Phase 2: Framework Development (4 Months)

Focus on establishing foundational structures:

- basic governance structures

- core decision frameworks

- essential stakeholder engagement

Phase 3: System Integration (4 Months)

Effective governance frameworks emerge through sustained attention to how data naturally flows through educational communities. Systems that adapt to changing needs while maintaining consistent protection enhance school communities (Schilhab & Groth 2024).

Extended Development (Years 2–3)

Building on the foundation established in Year 1:

- advanced governance systems

- comprehensive frameworks

- deep community involvement

Implementation Framework

A successful governance structure requires these key components:

- **Regular review cycles:**
    - monthly meetings with teacher representatives
    - quarterly reviews with parent advisory groups
    - annual comprehensive policy assessments

- **Feedback integration:**
    - clear channels for stakeholder input
    - documented process for evaluating suggestions
    - timeline requirements for responding to concerns

- **Adaptation protocols:**
    - framework for evaluating new data practices
    - process for updating existing policies
    - guidelines for emergency policy changes

This systematic approach ensures that

- Community voices actively shape data practices.
- Schools can respond quickly to new challenges.
- Educational goals remain the primary focus.
- Trust is maintained through transparent decision-making.

Quality data governance is about supporting student success while ensuring their well-being.

Effective data management is about building trust. The most successful programs make protection feel natural, seamlessly integrating security into daily school life.

The goal is to develop approaches that grow with your community's needs while maintaining an unwavering commitment to student protection. Living systems evolve while preserving essential safeguards.

Looking Ahead

Through thoughtful implementation, data protection is more than a legal requirement but a fundamental part of how schools support student learning. Keep your focus on educational benefits while ensuring robust protection, and let your governance systems strengthen your school's mission.

As we move into Chapter 8, we'll explore how to measure the success of these data management systems and make necessary adjustments based on real-world implementation experience. The journey of data management in embodied AI education continues to evolve but with careful attention to these principles, schools can create systems that both protect and empower their learning communities.

Chapter 8:

Discovering Success and Iterating

Every transformative experience begins with a simple question: "How do we know this is working?" In the world of educational AI, the answer emerges not just from data points and metrics, but from the daily rhythm of school life. Success reveals itself in subtle ways—a student moving naturally between embodied AI-supported learning stations, a teacher confidently adjusting instruction based on real-time insights, or a quiet moment when technology seems to disappear entirely, leaving only enhanced learning and unknown or unexpected potential for unique learning, a more enactive approach to adapting to a constantly changing living system.

Defining Success Metrics for Embodied AI Implementation

The journey of measuring AI's impact often begins by challenging traditional notions of success. One district discovered that their most meaningful metrics beyond utilizing standardized measures emerged from a more qualitative approach to observing how naturally students and teachers integrated AI into their daily learning experiences, teaching teachers how to observe learning. Learning how to observe is intertwined with the co-mingling or embodying AI strategies in each school system as a whole and individualized teacher classrooms. AI is not just for students but aids the teachers learning or teaching potential toward a pedagogy of success.

Success in AI integration transcends conventional benchmarks. Consider how one group of educators transformed their evaluation approach by first watching how learning actually happened in embodied AI-enhanced environments.

Exercise: Success Metric Evolution

Objective: Develop meaningful measures that capture both quantitative improvements and qualitative transformations in teaching and learning.

The Discovery Process (8 Weeks)

Month 1: Observation Phase

Begin by documenting the natural indicators of successful integration. Focus on moments when

- learning flows seamlessly between embodied AI-supported and traditional activities

- teachers instinctively foster AI insights to enhance instruction

- students engage naturally embodying AI-enhanced learning environments

- technology supports rather than disrupts classroom dynamics

Create what veteran educators call a "success journal," capturing detailed observations about

- How have patterns of student engagement transformed over time?

- In what ways have teaching practices evolved since implementation?

- Where do you notice shifts in your learning environment's dynamic flow?

- What unexpected positive outcomes and new ways of knowing have emerged?

Month 2: Framework Development

Transform these observations into what experienced integrators call "living metrics"—measures that evolve with your program while maintaining focus on meaningful outcomes and embodied interactions. Rather than simply tracking usage statistics or test scores, develop indicators that capture the depth and quality of embodied AI integration.

Exercise: Metric Development Workshop

Observation areas: Consider patterns of

- student agency in learning

- natural technology adoption

- opening spaces for potential, confidence, and growth

- community engagement levels

Document both visible changes and subtle shifts in

- classroom dynamics

- professional collaboration

- student independence

- enactive learning environment flexibility

Collecting and Analyzing Data on Embodied AI Integration

The art of gathering meaningful data about embodied AI integration emerged when educators started looking beyond traditional measurement approaches. They discovered that the most valuable insights often came from observing how teaching and learning naturally evolved in AI-enhanced environments.

Exercise: Integration Analysis Framework

Objective: Create a comprehensive yet natural approach to understanding AI's impact on your educational environment.

Gathering Baseline Insights

Begin with what experienced integrators call "environmental awareness"—developing a clear picture of your starting point through careful observation and documentation.

Documentation focus:

- current teaching patterns

- student learning behaviors

- community engagement levels

- professional development impact

Look especially for

- natural adoption patterns

- resistance points

- unexpected adaptations

- organic innovations

Analyzing Patterns

Review your documentation to identify

- recurring themes in teaching and learning

- moments of the highest engagement

- areas where support is most needed

- successful adaptation strategies

Planning Forward

Based on your insights

- identify priority areas for AI integration

- map potential implementation pathways

- determine necessary support structures

- outline professional development needs

Implementation Guidelines

Remember to

- build on existing strengths

- respect natural teaching rhythms

- maintain flexibility in approach

- regularly gather feedback

- adjust strategies based on observations

This framework serves as a living document—one that evolves with your community's journey into AI integration. By starting with careful observation and moving thoughtfully through analysis to action, you create space for organic growth while ensuring purposeful progress. Remember that the goal isn't perfect implementation, but rather meaningful integration that enhances your educational environment's natural strengths and learning rhythms.

Iterating and Improving Embodied AI Integration Strategies

The most successful embodied AI implementations grow through what veteran educators call "responsive iteration"—thoughtful adjustments based on real-world experiences rather than predetermined pathways. This approach transforms challenges into opportunities for growth and refinement.

Exercise: Strategic Iteration Process

Objective: Develop a flexible, responsive approach to improving AI integration based on authentic classroom experiences.

Implementation Cycle (Quarterly)

First Quarter: Deep Listening

Begin by gathering what experienced integrators call "ground truth"— the actual experiences of teachers, students, and staff working with AI systems daily (Tjandra et al., 2017). Rather than relying solely on usage data or satisfaction surveys, create opportunities for authentic feedback through

- informal observation sessions

- open dialogue meetings

- regular reflection circles

- hands-on workshops

Second Quarter: Pattern Recognition

Transform collected insights into actionable knowledge. Look for

- common success patterns

- shared challenges

- unexpected innovations

- natural adaptation strategies

Handling Challenges and Troubleshooting

Every AI implementation journey encounters obstacles. The key lies in embracing challenges as opportunities for enactive learning and system improvement. Success emerges from what seasoned educators call "productive problem-solving"—addressing issues while strengthening the overall integration process.

Exercise: Challenge Response Framework

Objective: Create a systematic yet flexible approach to addressing implementation challenges.

Initial assessment: Begin with what experienced integrators refer to as "challenge mapping"—understanding ways to change or discover even stronger or new ways of implementing learning experiences. Consider

- context of the challenge

- impact on learning

- available resources

- potential opportunities

Solution development: Work through challenges using what one technology coordinator termed "collaborative innovation"—bringing together different perspectives to develop effective solutions (Brown et al., 2021). Focus on

- quick wins for immediate relief

- long-term sustainable solutions

- preventive measures

- system improvements

Continuous Evaluation and Adjustment

Successful enactive learning while embodying AI implementation requires ongoing attention to the "living system" of technology integration. This means creating feedback loops that support continuous improvement while maintaining focus on educational goals.

Exercise: Continuous Improvement Cycle

Objective: Establish sustainable processes for ongoing evaluation and refinement of flow integration.

Implementation Structure (Annual Cycle)

Quarterly reviews: Plan milestone checkpoints, structured but natural opportunities to assess progress and plan improvements:

- **Fall quarter:**

    - establish baseline measures

    - set improvement goals

    - launch new initiatives

    - gather initial feedback

- **Winter quarter:**

    - analyze early results

    - make midcourse corrections

    - address emerging challenges

    - share successful strategies

- **Spring quarter:**

    - document growth patterns

    - identify summer goals

    - plan professional development

    - prepare for expansion

- **Summer quarter:**
  - deep dive analysis
  - strategic planning
  - system updates
  - preparation for the new year

Remember throughout this process that successful measurement and iteration depends on maintaining focus on what matters most—enriched spaces of potential teaching and learning. The most effective evaluation systems feel natural rather than imposed, generating insights that lead to meaningful pedagogy.

Consider creating "learning loops"—ongoing cycles of observation, reflection, and adjustment that become part of your school's natural rhythm. These loops should

- support authentic assessment
- encourage innovation
- address challenges promptly
- celebrate successes
- build community engagement

Through thoughtful enactive learning successes and iteration, embodying AI integration becomes a dynamic process of improvement continuously growing beyond a static implementation. Learning potential emerges in addition to executed plans from enactive learning to real-world experiences and needs.

Keep your focus on how embodied AI fosters a more embodied teaching and learning experience while maintaining flexibility in your approach to measurement and adjustment. The goal is continuous growth toward more effective and natural integration of embodied AI in education.

Chapter 9:

Advanced AI Applications in

Education

The future of education unfolds through the subtle interweaving of embodied AI with everyday learning experiences. In a classroom somewhere, a student moves naturally through a virtual ancient Rome, their gestures part of an unfolding body–mind–world experience. Across the globe, another classroom's enactive curriculum flows seamlessly based on observed learning patterns. These possibilities represent the emerging potential of embodied AI in education, where the lines between being and knowing blur in moments of deep engagement.

Global Learning Ecosystems

Consider the possibilities when classrooms across continents connect through embodied AI:

- A nature class in Finland shares environmental observations with students in Brazil.

- Mathematics students in Japan and Canada explore geometric concepts through shared movement.

- Art classes in South Africa and Mexico cocreate through gesture-based interactions.

These cross-cultural connections create "global flow pedagogy"—learning experiences that transcend traditional boundaries while remaining deeply embodied.

Embodied AI and Flow Pedagogy in Curriculum Design

The evolution of curriculum design emerges from amplifying educators' natural ability to recognize and interact with student potential. Through global classroom partnerships, teachers discover how shared embodied AI experiences create unique opportunities for the coevolution of teaching and learning practices.

Dynamic Flow Pedagogy Development

Imagine science classes across continents sharing

- students' natural movement patterns during experiments

- spontaneous physical demonstrations of concepts

- cultural variations in embodied understanding

- moments where learning transcends traditional boundaries

These shared observations inform "flow ecosystems"—learning spaces where embodied AI supports natural learning rhythms across diverse contexts.

Exercise: Cross-Cultural Curriculum Evolution

Objective: Create living curriculum frameworks that adapt to unique cultural and environmental contexts while fostering universal learning potentials.

Development Journey (One Semester)

Month 1: Global Pattern Recognition

- Partner with classrooms in different contexts (urban/rural, indoor/outdoor, or various cultures).

- Document how learning naturally unfolds in each environment.

- Notice universal patterns in body–mind engagement.

- Identify cultural variations in physical expression.

For example, one outdoor education program partnered with an urban classroom to explore

- how different environments unleash movement patterns

- ways students naturally demonstrate understanding

- cultural variations in gesture and expression

- moments of shared discovery across contexts

Month 2: Flow Integration Design

Transform these observations into "adaptive flow pathways"—curriculum frameworks that

- Honor cultural differences in embodied learning.

- Support natural movement patterns.

- Foster unexpected learning moments.

- Create spaces for shared discovery.

Research opportunity: This framework offers rich potential for graduate research exploring

- cross-cultural patterns in embodied learning

- environmental influences on movement and understanding

- universal aspects of physical demonstration

- cultural variations in fostering flow

Human Potential and Predictive Flow Models

Let's consider how embodied AI can help us recognize and nurture moments of deep engagement—or "flow experiences" in learning. Through international collaboration, educators discover patterns of body–mind integration that transcend cultural boundaries.

Exercise: Flow Pattern Recognition

Objective: Create systems that recognize and support natural learning rhythms across diverse contexts.

Implementation Process (3 Months)

Phase 1: Global Pattern Documentation

Partner with international educators to observe

- universal indicators of deep engagement

- cultural variations in learning expression

- environmental influences on movement patterns

- shared moments of discovery

Research opportunity: Graduate students might explore

- how flow states manifest across cultures

- environmental impacts on embodied learning

- universal patterns in physical understanding

- cultural variations in learning rhythms

Phase 2: Flow System Integration

Create "flow support frameworks" that

- honor cultural learning patterns

- support environmental adaptation

- foster unexpected discoveries

- enable cross-cultural connection

Immersive Body–Mind–World Experiences

The potential of immersive learning emerges when technology disappears into the background, leaving only the pure experience of body–mind–world integration. Through international collaboration, we discover how different cultures naturally explore and understand through enactive learning.

Exercise: Global Learning Environment Development

Objective: Create immersive experiences that support natural learning behaviors across cultures.

Cross-Cultural Movement Mapping

Work with international partners to document natural learning patterns and expressions across diverse educational settings.

Documentation focus:

- universal exploration patterns

- cultural variations in movement

- environmental influences on learning

- shared moments of discovery

Pattern Recognition

Analyze observations to identify

- common learning movements across cultures

- unique cultural approaches to knowledge-sharing

- environmental design influences

- successful cross-cultural adaptations

Design Integration

Based on insights

- develop flexible learning spaces

- incorporate culturally responsive elements

- create adaptable teaching approaches

- build inclusive movement opportunities

Remember to

- honor cultural authenticity

- maintain local context

- encourage organic adaptation

- facilitate cross-cultural dialogue

- document emerging practices

By observing and integrating diverse ways of knowing and showing understanding, we create learning environments that celebrate both our universal human connection to movement and our beautiful cultural differences in expressing knowledge.

Natural Language Flow in Learning Environments

The evolution of language interaction in education transcends simple dialogue systems, moving toward "flow conversations"—natural exchanges that emerge when body, mind, and world align in moments of shared understanding. Through international partnerships, we discover how embodied communication transcends cultural and linguistic boundaries.

Exercise: Global Communication Flow Development

Objective: Explore and enhance cross-cultural communication through movement and embodied learning.

Cross-Cultural Interaction Analysis

Partner with international classrooms to document and understand physical expression in learning.

Documentation focus:

- universal patterns in physical communication

- cultural variations in gesture and movement

- shared moments of understanding

- body–mind expression across languages

Research observations:

- how meaning flows through movement

- universal gestures in learning

- cultural variations in embodied expression

- cross-cultural learning patterns

Pattern Recognition

Analyze documented interactions to identify

- common physical expressions across cultures

- unique cultural communication styles

- universal understanding moments

- successful bridging strategies

Communication Integration

Based on insights

- develop inclusive gesture vocabularies

- create cross-cultural movement activities

- design universal communication tools

- build movement-based learning experiences

Implementation Guidelines

Remember to

- respect cultural differences

- celebrate shared expressions

- encourage organic development

- document emerging patterns

- maintain cultural sensitivity

Through careful observation and thoughtful integration, we discover how physical expression can bridge linguistic boundaries and create deeper understanding across global learning communities. These insights help us build more inclusive and expressive learning environments that celebrate both our shared humanity and our rich cultural diversity.

Emerging Possibilities in Embodied AI

The landscape continues to evolve, yet core principles remain: technology should support the natural flow of body–mind–world integration, foster unexpected discoveries, and create spaces for learning potential to emerge naturally.

Exercise: Global Innovation Flow Framework

Implementation Structure

Phase 1: Cross-Cultural Assessment

Begin with a "flow-first evaluation":

- How does the technology support natural learning rhythms?

- Does it foster unexpected discoveries?

- Can it adapt to different cultural contexts?

- Does it enable meaningful cross-cultural connection?

Phase 2: Global Pilot Development

Create flexible approaches through

- international learning partnerships

- cross-cultural exploration

- shared discovery documentation

- collaborative research opportunities

Throughout this journey, remember that the deepest learning often happens in those moments when time seems to stop, when the boundaries between student, teacher, and environment blur in what we might call "flow mindset" of understanding. Success emerges when

- Learning transcends traditional boundaries.

- Cultural wisdom enhances shared understanding.

- Unexpected discoveries emerge naturally.

- Body–mind–world integration occurs spontaneously.

The future lies in creating spaces where embodied AI and human wisdom work together, enhancing learning across cultures and contexts. Focus on

- fostering universal learning patterns

- honoring cultural variations

- supporting unexpected discoveries

- creating spaces for flow experiences

Through thoughtful implementation and global collaboration, we create learning environments that combine cultural wisdom with technological potential. True success reveals itself in those unique moments when the lines between teaching and learning dissolve, and pure discovery emerges through the natural flow of body–mind–world interaction.

The most sophisticated implementations often feel the most natural— their value fostered through the depth of learning experiences and moments of pure engagement they enable. Let this understanding guide your exploration of embodied AI's potential in education.

Chapter 10:

Future-Proofing Your Embodiment

of AI Integration

The most resilient approaches to embodied AI in education emerge from flexible foundations that adapt to evolving learning potentials. When educational institutions build these adaptable systems, they create environments where innovation flourishes naturally. Through global collaboration and shared discovery, learning communities worldwide embrace new possibilities while maintaining a focus on fundamental learning principles.

The Rhythm of Global Learning Networks

Education transcends traditional boundaries in today's interconnected world, creating a continuous flow of learning that follows the sun across continents. This natural progression allows insights to develop and mature as they travel across time zones, enriched by each culture they touch.

Morning Discovery Sessions: Global Sharing

European educators initiate the daily cycle, bringing fresh perspectives as their day begins. Their early observations often focus on

- emerging patterns from the previous day's implementation

- fresh insights from overnight reflection

- new approaches ready for testing

- questions that arose during planning

As the day progresses, Asian colleagues enter the flow:

- building upon European discoveries

- adding cultural perspectives

- sharing implementation experiences

- contributing unique adaptations

American teachers join next, bringing

- fresh energy to ongoing discussions

- new implementation contexts

- cultural variations on shared themes

- innovative adaptation strategies

Australian peers complete the cycle by

- synthesizing global insights

- testing adapted approaches

- documenting emerging patterns

- preparing for the next cycle

These natural rhythms foster global flow awareness—the ability to recognize and adapt to emerging possibilities across cultural contexts. This awareness transforms isolated innovations into shared wisdom, enriched by diverse perspectives and experiences.

Building Sustainable Implementation Cycles

From this foundation of global connection emerges a natural quarterly rhythm of growth and development. Each quarter builds upon the previous one, creating a spiral of continuous improvement and innovation.

First Quarter: Vision and Connection

The journey begins with relationship building and vision development:

- Establish international partnerships that spark innovation:

    o   Identify complementary strengths.

    o   Create communication protocols.

    o   Build trust through small collaborations.

    o   Develop shared language for innovation.

- Begin local vision mapping to ground global insights:

    o   Document current practices.

    o   Identify growth opportunities.

    o   Map potential connections.

    o   Plan initial experiments.

- Document emerging patterns across cultures:

    o   Note successful adaptation strategies.

    o   Track innovation flow.

    o   Identify cultural variations.

- Record unexpected discoveries.

- Create sharing spaces that nurture collaboration:

  - Design flexible meeting structures.

  - Establish documentation systems.

  - Build communication channels.

  - Develop feedback loops.

As these initial connections take root, the second quarter opens new possibilities for deeper implementation.

Second Quarter: Implementation Flow

Building on established relationships, communities begin active experimentation:

- Start small adaptations based on shared insights:

  - Test promising approaches.

  - Document early results.

  - Gather feedback.

  - Make rapid adjustments.

- Observe natural patterns as they emerge:

  - Track successful variations.

  - Note cultural influences.

  - Document adaptation strategies.

  - Identify growth indicators.

- Share early discoveries across networks:

  - Celebrate small successes.

  - Learn from challenges.

  - Build collective wisdom.

  - Inspire new experiments.

- Support organic growth within communities:

  - Nurture emerging leaders.

  - Strengthen connections.

  - Deepen understanding.

  - Expand possibilities.

This phase of active experimentation naturally leads to deeper pattern recognition in the third quarter.

Third Quarter: Pattern Recognition

As implementation experience deepens, communities develop a more sophisticated understanding:

- Identify successful adaptations across contexts:

  - Map effective practices.

  - Understand cultural variations.

  - Document success factors.

  - Track growth indicators.

- Document unexpected discoveries that emerge:

    ○ Capture innovation patterns.

    ○ Note surprising connections.

    ○ Record unplanned benefits.

    ○ Track emergent possibilities.

- Share emerging insights throughout networks:

    ○ Connect related discoveries.

    ○ Build collective understanding.

    ○ Develop shared language.

    ○ Create resource collections.

- Deepen global connections through shared learning:

    ○ Strengthen partnerships.

    ○ Expand collaboration.

    ○ Integrate perspectives.

    ○ Plan future growth.

The final quarter synthesizes these learnings while preparing for future development.

Fourth Quarter: Evolution and Planning

Communities consolidate learning while building foundations for continued growth:

- Synthesize yearly learning across networks:

    o Identify key patterns.

    o Document best practices.

    o Map innovation pathways.

    o Create resource libraries.

- Refine vision through collective experience:

    o Update growth plans.

    o Adjust strategies.

    o Incorporate new insights.

    o Expand possibilities.

- Strengthen global partnerships for future growth:

    o Deepen connections.

    o Plan joint projects.

    o Create support structures.

    o Build sustainability.

Sustaining Growth Through Natural Rhythms

The sustainability of these networks depends on establishing natural cycles of learning and sharing. Through embodied resilience, communities develop their own rhythms of growth that support continuous development.

Weekly flow rhythms: Each day builds through a natural progression:

- Morning global connections spark new insights:

  - Share recent discoveries.

  - Pose emerging questions.

  - Plan daily experiments.

  - Build collective energy.

- Midday implementation brings ideas to life:

  - Test new approaches.

  - Document results.

  - Make quick adjustments.

  - Support innovation.

- Afternoon reflection deepens understanding:

  - Review outcomes.

  - Identify patterns.

  - Share initial insights.

  - Plan refinements.

- Evening documentation preserves discoveries:

  - Record key learnings.

  - Connect related insights.

  - Prepare for sharing.

  - Set up the next cycle.

These organic patterns support flow consciousness, creating spaces where unexpected discoveries flourish and learning communities thrive.

Vision-Based Growth in Practice

As learning communities mature, their growth patterns naturally expand through flow networks. Each environment cultivates unique approaches shaped by local conditions and global connections.

Community Foundations

- Vision and values guide development:

    o Shared purpose drives growth.

    o Cultural wisdom informs practice.

    o Collective aspirations shape direction.

    o Individual goals enrich the community.

- Cultural context enriches learning:

    o Local traditions provide a foundation.

    o Global perspectives add depth.

    o Diverse approaches spark innovation.

    o Unique expressions flourish.

- Physical and virtual spaces support connection:

    o Flexible environments enable collaboration.

    o Digital tools bridge distances.

- Hybrid spaces blend approaches.

- Natural flow emerges.

- Resources and connections enable growth:

  - Local assets support development.

  - Global networks provide resources.

  - Partnerships expand possibilities.

  - Innovation flourishes naturally.

Monthly Cycles of Discovery Flow

The journey unfolds through three distinct yet interconnected phases, each building on the previous while preparing for the next.

Month 1: Vision Exploration

Communities begin by grounding their work in shared purpose:

- Nurture personal learning aspirations:

  - Identify individual goals.

  - Connect to collective vision.

  - Support growth pathways.

  - Celebrate diversity.

- Cultivate community dreams:

  - Build shared vision.

- o   Map possibilities.

- o   Plan initial steps.

- o   Create support structures.

- Honor cultural values:

  - o   Integrate traditions.

  - o   Respect diversity.

  - o   Build inclusion.

  - o   Support expression.

- Welcome unexpected possibilities:

  - o   Remain open to discovery.

  - o   Embrace emergence.

  - o   Support innovation.

  - o   Celebrate surprises.

Month 2: Pattern Recognition

Building on initial vision work, communities deepen their practice:

- Document natural learning rhythms and student engagement patterns across different times and activities.

- Observe how physical space, movement, and teaching approaches influence learning momentum.

- Map which experiences consistently spark meaningful discussions and deeper student exploration.

- Track transitions and interactions that flow naturally versus those that create friction.

Month 3: Flow Integration

Communities move into deeper implementation:

- Deepen global connections:
    - Strengthen partnerships.
    - Expand networks.
    - Share resources.
    - Build sustainability.
- Expand local initiatives:
    - Scale successful practices.
    - Adapt to new contexts.
    - Support innovation.
    - Build capacity.
- Share emerging insights:
    - Document learning.
    - Create resources.
    - Support adoption.
    - Foster collaboration.

The Magic of Flow Consciousness

In discovery spaces, learning spreads naturally through communities (Acomi et al., 2023). These vibrant environments foster continuous development through multiple dimensions.

Personal Growth Dimensions

- Exploration ignites development:

    o individual discoveries

    o skill development

    o confidence building

    o vision expansion

- Cultural expression enriches understanding:

    o traditional wisdom

    o contemporary adaptations

    o creative innovations

    o unique perspectives

Collective Development Paths

- Collaborative discovery sparks innovation:

    o shared experiments

    o combined insights

    o joint projects

- collective wisdom

- Continuous evolution sustains growth:

    - regular reflection

    - adaptive planning

    - responsive adjustment

    - forward movement

Cultural Enrichment Through Natural Growth

Global learning communities thrive through the diversity of approaches and perspectives.

Cultural Contributions

- Multiple paths to success:

    - different measures

    - varied approaches

    - unique indicators

    - diverse celebrations

- Natural development rhythms:

    - cultural cycles

    - traditional patterns

    - modern adaptations

    - blended approaches

Future Vision Development

Learning awareness emerges through recognizing and adapting to unfolding potentials (Muukkonen & Kajamaa, 2024). Each community develops unique patterns while contributing to collective wisdom.

Growth Indicators

- Community aspirations drive development:
  - shared goals
  - collective vision
  - united action
  - common purpose
- Cultural values enrich understanding:
  - traditional wisdom
  - modern insights
  - blended approaches
  - innovation paths

Seasonal Rhythms of Growth

Learning communities follow natural cycles that support sustained development.

Fall: Renewal and Connection

- Vision renewal energizes growth:

    - fresh perspectives

    - new possibilities

    - clear direction

    - strong purpose

- Connection building strengthens communities:

    - new partnerships

    - deeper relationships

    - expanded networks

    - enhanced collaboration

Winter: Deep Implementation

- Implementation grounds learning:

    - practical application

    - real-world testing

    - concrete results

    - clear feedback

- Reflection deepens understanding:

    - pattern recognition

    - insight development

- o knowledge integration

- o wisdom building

Spring: Adaptation and Growth

- Recognition of patterns:

  - o success factors

  - o growth indicators

  - o challenge points

  - o innovation opportunities

- Innovation blooms:

  - o new approaches

  - o fresh perspectives

  - o creative solutions

  - o expanded possibilities

Summer: Celebration and Planning

- Celebration of journeys:

  - o acknowledged growth

  - o shared successes

  - o learned lessons

  - o community achievements

- Evolution planning:
  - future vision
  - next steps
  - resource development
  - capacity building

Looking Forward to Flow Pedagogy

Creating spaces where embodied learning flourishes becomes a natural extension of educational practice. These environments support discovery, nurture growth, and celebrate unique contributions from every community member. As we move into exploring specific classroom practices, these principles will guide our understanding of how global patterns manifest in local contexts.

The success of these learning ecosystems emerges through

- mindful attention to natural rhythms

- support for organic development

- celebration of diverse approaches

- continuous adaptation and growth

- a deep connection to community wisdom

Together, these elements create rich environments where learning flows naturally, innovation thrives, and communities grow stronger through shared discovery and collective wisdom.

Conclusion

The journey of integrating embodied AI into education resembles less a straight path and more an intricate web of potential, where each learning moment contributes to an unfolding space of human possibility. Throughout this book, we've explored how thoughtful implementation emerges through embodying and nurturing the natural rhythms of teaching and learning.

Enacting Learning Success Through Embodied AI

Success emerges through flow pedagogy—the mindful balance between embracing new possibilities while preserving effective practices. The most successful implementations share common elements: they grow organically from existing strengths, support natural teaching patterns, and create spaces where mind–body–world AI experiences unfold naturally.

Key insights reveal that effective integration

- begins with understanding your community's unique vision and potential

- builds on existing teaching wisdom

- develops through enactive learning networks

- succeeds through community engagement and shared discovery

- grows through attention to unexpected possibilities

Initial Actions for Your Journey

Begin with going beyond just technology selection but with community visioning. Start by gathering your "enactive learning circle"—a diverse group who can help guide your learning environment's evolution. Begin with small, meaningful steps that build confidence and potential.

First steps:

1. Map your current learning landscape.

2. Build your global support network.

3. Start small but dream expansively.

4. Document unexpected discoveries.

5. Celebrate emerging possibilities.

Creating Sustainable Growth

The path of embodied AI integration requires ongoing exploration and discovery. Success emerges through "enactive learning networks" — connections that support continuous growth and development.

Consider developing

- global learning communities focused on embodied AI

- partnerships across diverse learning environments

- connections with researchers and practitioners

- regular exploration of emerging possibilities

- ways of sharing unexpected discoveries

Enjoy the journey as the magic happens in the messy interspaces where potential and thoughtful exploration enhance teaching and learning while maintaining focus on what matters most: creating spaces where human potential can flourish in natural and meaningful ways.

Your path will be unique to your community, emerging from your particular vision and values. Let your implementation grow organically from your environment's needs and aspirations, always focusing on how embodied AI can enhance and support the natural unfolding of human potential.

The future of embodied AI in education will be written by those who understand that success comes from continuous exploration of technology while creating spaces where learning naturally emerges through the integration of mind, body, and world experiences.

The richness of this journey reveals itself in unexpected moments—when a student discovers a new way of demonstrating understanding through movement, when teachers spontaneously share breakthroughs during morning coffee, and when the administration and staff collectively witness learning transforming through the thoughtful integration of embodied AI. These moments, though impossible to plan, emerge naturally when we create the right conditions for growth and discovery.

Consider this book not as an endpoint but as an invitation to explore the vast potential that lies at the intersection of human learning and technological support. Just as a garden provides structure while allowing for natural growth, your implementation of embodied AI should offer a framework while celebrating organic development and unexpected flourishing.

As you move forward, remain attentive to

- the natural rhythms of your learning community

- the wisdom embedded in current practices

- the potential for unexpected connections

- the power of patient, organic growth

- the importance of celebrating small victories

Remember that the most profound transformations often begin quietly—in a moment of student insight, in a spontaneous collaboration between colleagues, and an unexpected application of familiar tools. By maintaining a balance between structured support and organic growth and between technological enhancement and human wisdom, you create space for these transformative moments to emerge and multiply.

Your journey with embodied AI continues beyond these pages, unfolding in ways unique to your learning community. Trust in the process, honor the wisdom of your colleagues, and remain open to the possibilities that emerge when we create spaces where technology enhances our journey of human potential. The future of education lies in intentional implementation and thoughtful integration that honors both the future and tradition, both structure and spontaneity, and both technology and human connection.

About the Author

Johnna Haskell is an adventurer at heart, looking for transformative experiences in pedagogy, sports, flying, and everyday life.

Johnna has a PhD in curriculum studies/science education with extensive research in flow pedagogy of outdoor education. She completed her MSEd in educational leadership. She attained her BS degree in animal science while minoring in studio art and outdoor education.

Johnna's work concentrates on flow pedagogy and the outdoor embodied experience. Johnna's broad depth of experience includes freelance wildlife photographer, science educator, administrator, and university teacher for over 18 years in education before shifting her passion back to sharing her extensive perspectives on the body–mind–world.

She has explored the outdoors via canoes, kayaks, skis, rock and ice climbing, backpacking, mountaineering, and paragliding. Her pursuits have included climbing the ascents of Denali (20,320 ft) and an attempt to paraglide off the summit of Kilimanjaro (19,341 ft) for a major charity event to help with water supplies in various African communities.

Did You Enjoy Reading Embodied

AI Integration in Education?

Thank you for joining me on this journey through embodied AI integration in education. I hope this guide has sparked new possibilities for your teaching practice.

If you found value in *Embodied AI Integration in Education: A Thoughtful Implementation Guide for Innovative Teaching* and feel it has enhanced your understanding of AI implementation, I would be deeply grateful if you would consider sharing your thoughts in a brief Amazon review. Even a few sentences about what resonated with you could help other educators discover these transformative approaches.

Your perspective matters—authentic feedback from practicing educators helps colleagues make informed decisions about their professional development resources.

To stay updated on new releases and access early-bird pricing, please join our learning community at www.epicleafinnovations.com. Our community thrives on the exchange of ideas and practical experiences, and I'd love for you to be part of this ongoing conversation about the future of education. Please scan the QR codes below to:

Join the mailing list!   Leave us a review!

Have implementation stories to share or questions to explore? I'd love to hear from you at info@epicleafinnovations.com

With gratitude for your commitment to evolving education,

Johnna Haskell

References

Acomi, N., Acomi, O., Akceviz Ova, N., Akilli, A., Anlar, E., Martínez, H. B., Arisoy, P., Necmeddin, M., Kurt, H., Marzano, F., Nur Akarcay, Y., Ochoa Sigüencia, L., Pelligrino, A., Yucel, Ö., & Zorzi, S. (2023). Creativity and arts in digital social innovation. *Zenodo.* https://doi.org/10.5281/zenodo.8052835

Agyeman, N., Y., & Aphane, V. (2024). Exploring school leadership styles used to improve instruction and learning in schools. *Journal of Research Initiatives, 8*(3), Article 1. https://files.eric.ed.gov/fulltext/EJ1435342.pdf

Akram, H., Abdelrady, A. H., Al-Adwan, A. S., & Ramzan, M. (2022). Teachers' perceptions of technology integration in teaching-learning practices: A systematic review. *Frontiers in Psychology, 13*(1), Article 920317. https://doi.org/10.3389/fpsyg.2022.920317

Almasri, F. (2024). Exploring the impact of artificial intelligence in teaching and learning of science: A systematic review of empirical research. *International Journal of Educational Technology in Higher Education, 54*, 977–997. https://doi.org/10.1007/s11165-024-10176-3

Bond, M., Buntins, K., Bedenlier, S., Zawacki-Richter, O., & Kerres, M. (2020). Mapping research in student engagement and educational technology in higher education: a systematic evidence map. *International Journal of Educational Technology in Higher Education, 17*(1), 1–30. https://doi.org/10.1186/s41239-019-0176-8

Brown, P., Von Daniels, C., Bocken, N. M. P., & Balkenende, A. R. (2021). A process model for collaboration in circular oriented innovation. *Journal of Cleaner Production, 286*, Article 125499. https://doi.org/10.1016/j.jclepro.2020.125499

Cohen, M., Rohan, A., Pritchard, K., & Pettit, K. (2022). *Guide to data chats: Convening community conversations about data.* Urban Institute. https://www.urban.org/sites/default/files/2022-06/Guide%20to%20Data%20Chats_%20Convening%20Community%20Conversations%20about%20Data.pdf

Coursera. (n.d.). *Artificial intelligence education for teachers.* https://www.coursera.org/learn/artificial-intelligence-education-for-teachers

Giannakos, M. N., Sharma, K., Pappas, I. O., Kostakos, V., & Velloso, E. (2019). Multimodal data as a means to understand the learning experience. *International Journal of Information Management, 48*, 108–119. https://doi.org/10.1016/j.ijinfomgt.2019.02.003

Goh, T.-T., & Yang, B. (2021). The role of e-engagement and flow on the continuance with a learning management system in a blended learning environment. *International Journal of Educational Technology in Higher Education, 18*(1). https://doi.org/10.1186/s41239-021-00285-8

Hwang, G.-J., & Chen, N.-S. (2024). Exploring the potential of generative artificial intelligence in education: Applications, challenges, and future research directions. *Educational Technology & Society, 26*(2). https://doi.org/10.30191/ETS.202304_26(2).0014

International Society for Technology in Education. (n.d.). *Artificial intelligence in education.* https://iste.org/ai

Martinez, C. (2022). Developing 21st century teaching skills: A case study of teaching and learning through project-based curriculum. *Cogent Education, 9*(1), 1–16. https://doi.org/10.1080/2331186x.2021.2024936

Muukkonen, H., & Kajamaa, A. (2024). Knowledge objects and knowledge practices in interdisciplinary learning: Example of an organization simulation in higher education. *Journal of the Learning Sciences, 33*(2), 1–40. https://doi.org/10.1080/10508406.2024.2344794

National Forum on Education Statistics. (2016). *Forum guide to education data privacy.* (NFES 2016-096). U.S. Department of Education.

Nguyen, A., Tuunanen, T., Gardner, L., & Sheridan, D. (2020). Design principles for learning analytics information systems in higher education. *European Journal of Information Systems, 30*(5), 541–568. https://doi.org/10.1080/0960085x.2020.1816144

Schilhab, T., & Groth, C. (2024). Embodied Learning and Teaching using the 4E Cognition approach: *Exploring perspectives in teaching practices* (1st ed.). Routledge. https://doi.org/10.4324/9781003341604

Song, D. (2018). Learning analytics as an educational research approach. *International Journal of Multiple Research Approaches, 10*(1), 102–111. https://doi.org/10.29034/ijmra.v10n1a6

Tjandra, A., Sakti, S., & Nakamura, S. (2017, December 1). *Listening while speaking: Speech chain by deep learning.* 2017 IEEE Automatic Speech Recognition and Understanding Workshop (ASRU), Okinawa, Japan, 2017 (pp. 301–308). https://doi.org/10.1109/ASRU.2017.8268950

UNESCO. (2019). *Artificial intelligence in education.* https://www.unesco.org/en/digital-education/artificial-intelligence

Zhang, K., & Aslan, A. B. (2021). AI technologies for education: Recent research & future directions. *Computers and Education: Artificial Intelligence, 2,* Article 100025. https://doi.org/10.1016/j.caeai.2021.100025

www.ingramcontent.com/pod-product-compliance
Lightning Source LLC
Chambersburg PA
CBHW071146120626
46546CB00006B/2140